www.kamerabooks.co.uk

Colin Odell & Michelle Le Blanc

DAVID LYNCH

Kamera
BOOKS

First published in 2007 by Kamera Books
PO Box 394, Harpenden, Herts, AL5 1XJ
www.kamerabooks.co.uk

A CIP catalogue record for this book is available from the British Library.

ISBN-10: 1-84243-225-7
ISBN-13: 978-1-84243-225-9

Typeset by Avocet Typeset, Chilton, Aylesbury, Bucks
Printed by SNP Lefung Printers (Shenzen) Co Ltd, China

To the memory of Joan Le Blanc, a grand grandmother.

ACKNOWLEDGEMENTS

Our thanks to the usual suspects Lizbeth, Paul and Andrew for everything from fresh fish to accountancy, gigs and evenings at the pub. Thanks also to all the people who gave us a welcome respite from the PC during the writing of this book: Hanako & Gavin, Martin & Rosy, John & Michelle, Tarek, Julie, Yasmin, Dalia & Youssef and Arnis. Our love and thanks to Christine, Tony and Marc Le Blanc and to Truus Odell for all their support in a year of big changes. Thanks to the Kamera crew – Hannah, Elsa, Antonio and Ion. Finally to Alice. And Celia.

Special thanks to Barry Gifford and Oscar Bucher, who were so generous with their time.

CONTENTS

INTRODUCTION: THROUGH THE DARKNESS OF FUTURES PAST

'See that clock on the wall? In five minutes you are not going to
believe what I just told you...'[1]

In the territory between light and dark, between sleeping and waking,
there lies the world of David Lynch. It is a frightening and wonderful
place, full of mystery and discovery, of hopes and fears, and dreaming.
Always dreaming.

David Lynch's films contain some of the most distinguishing images
to grace the screen, both silver and small. As an artist who also works
in the media his output displays a singular worldview, both distinctive
and idiosyncratic in a marketplace over-burdened by mediocrity and
trends. Although this has gained him considerable critical acclaim,
including a *Palme d'Or*, the *Légion d'honneur* and a *Leone d'Oro* (Golden
Lion), it has also meant that funding and backing have on occasion
proved challenging. Key to his ability to engage an audience is the
symbiosis between sound and vision. The sound design in all of his work
is exemplary but also unconventional, often creating an ambient mood
that complements the picture or a sense of menace or wonder.

Many of Lynch's films deal in mysteries, either in the conventional
sense or through the unravelling of dreams, and often both simultaneously. His main protagonists frequently hide their curiosity for the darker
side of life beneath a veneer of wholesomeness. In this respect they are
representations of Lynch himself – the all-American Eagle Scout of the

idyllic rural US, fracturing society's fragile shell to find the rancour within. The line between despair and desire can be paper-thin. Rather like director Tod Browning, Lynch has an affinity with unconventional characters. His adoption of unusual individuals to populate his films – sometimes ordinary people he's found on set – is not a simple one of exploitation, nor is it one of identification. Instead there is a revelling in the diversity of humanity in all its shapes and forms, allowing him a wider palette to play upon. Unlike the work of Tim Burton, say, in which the abnormal is lauded, Lynch offers us a more realistic overview where there is good and evil in everyone regardless of their appearance.

As America's most high-profile purveyor of the surreal and an empathiser with the Surrealist movement, Lynch is not, as is commonly held, just a creator of the bizarre or macabre but a realiser of the subconscious. Dreams reveal the subconscious desires and fears of the dreamer and as such, no matter how outré, have their origins in the everyday. What Lynch brings to his works is not only a dreamlike state, half remembered in the haze of the morning, but also the absurdity of the mundane. In most film and television work, even long-running soap operas, the actuality of life, with its slow pace and coincidences, is often compressed for the sake of narrative convenience. Whilst such devices are necessary to all of Lynch's work, what really marks him out is his ability to pause the narrative thrust demanded in conventional Hollywood storytelling and observe the veracity of life in sometimes painful, raw close-up. The cinema of David Lynch is one where emotion and feeling rule over logic and reason. This is counter to the Freudian assertion that dreams fulfil wishes (even at a buried level) and that they are representative of the existence of the unconscious mind. In Lynch's world dreams are the doorway to a greater consciousness beyond conventional understanding – rather than being metaphors for our waking existence they are keys to a greater mystery and a wider being. Dreams do not reflect our world; they expand it and in some cases invade it.

David Lynch's world lies on the border between absurdity and reason, where the surreal invades the mundane. It is a strange and mysterious place but also a rewarding one where the barriers of reality have crumbled away. So join us on a journey to a land where creamed corn is scary, where robins bring dreams, where ugly is beautiful and there's always music in the air.

CAREER OVERVIEW – DAVID LYNCH, EAGLE SCOUT, MISSOULA, MONTANA

David Keith Lynch was born in Missoula, Montana on 20 January 1946, the eldest of three children. His father was a research scientist who worked for the Department of Forestry, which meant that David spent much of his childhood travelling around the country. Lynch has since described his upbringing as idyllic. 'It was a dream world of droning airplanes, blue skies, picket fences, green grass, cherry trees.'[2] He was popular at High School and successful in the Scout movement, becoming an Eagle Scout, and was present at John F Kennedy's inauguration. It was in the early 1960s that he became interested in art, partly through meeting the artist Bushnell Keeler. 'It happened in the front yard of my girlfriend Linda Styles's house in 1961. There was a guy there named Toby Keeler. He said, "My father is a painter": that completely changed everything. I was always drawing and painting but I thought it was something kids did. But at that moment I realised you could actually be a painter.'[3] Lynch rented a small portion of Keeler's studio and devoted himself to art along with his friend Jack Fisk, who would later play an important part in most of the director's productions. After school he enrolled at the Boston Museum School of Art but that turned out to be a mistake, as did a planned three-year trip around Europe. Lynch had intended to study with expressionist painter Oskar Kokoschka, but found that the artist was not at home in Salzburg, and so returned to America. Following a burst of creativity, he enrolled at the Pennsylvania Academy of the Fine Arts in Philadelphia, where he developed his own style of painting and also created mechanical sculptures. It was this progression to moving art that led him into film, aware that there were limits in the portrayal of movement on static canvas. Lynch created his first film with Jack Fisk, a one-minute loop called *Six Figures Getting Sick*, which was part film and part sculpture.

After seeing *Six Figures Getting Sick*, wealthy acquaintance H Barton Wasserman approached Lynch to make a similar film for his personal collection. Lynch purchased a camera and spent hours figuring out the intricacies of cinematography. He animated the entire film only to discover, on developing, that there was a camera fault and the whole thing was worthless. His generous benefactor was not unduly distressed, however, and allowed Lynch to use the rest of the money to make *The Alphabet*, a short film comprising live action as well as animation. Featuring Lynch's wife Peggy as The Girl, the film shows a number of disturbing animated images set to the chanting of the *Alphabet Song*.

By now, Lynch was becoming extremely interested in film as a medium, but could not afford to pursue his goals. It was only after Bushnell Keeler told him about the newly formed American Film Institute that he submitted a 'script' consisting of ideas and images along with *The Alphabet* and was awarded a grant. The result was *The Grandmother*, a disturbing tale of a boy so cruelly neglected by his parents that he decides to grow his own grandmother. Lynch won himself a place at the American Film Institute's Center for Advanced Film Studies and, with some assistance from the Institute and his close friends, began work on a feature-length picture. His dedication to the project was remarkable; he didn't start shooting until after two years into pre-production. Times were tough and he had to take several jobs to support himself, his wife and new daughter, including delivering the *Wall Street Journal* and building sheds. But the final result was to be one of the most remarkable debut features ever.

Eraserhead has often been cited as autobiographical. While still at art college, Lynch married his pregnant girlfriend. Yet this interpretation reads too much into the film. Lynch's extreme vision exaggerates and accentuates feelings, situations and emotions, but shouldn't necessarily be taken as a direct reflection of his life. He himself has stated that a baby may well have been the last thing he wanted at the time, but he has never regretted what happened. However, it was during the filming of *Eraserhead* that his marriage did finally break up, a casualty of the stress of trying to produce a film over such a long period of time. Lynch remarried in 1977, to Jack Fisk's sister Mary. *Eraserhead* was not an overnight success but it became popular on the cult circuit and its reputation grew by word of mouth. Producer Stuart Cornfeld was looking for a director to make a film about the Elephant Man for Mel Brooks' new company Brooksfilms and was so astonished by *Eraserhead* that he insisted Brooks attend a viewing. When Brooks emerged from the screening, he hugged the startled director and announced, 'You're a madman! I love you. You're in.'[4] Lynch was given complete control over *The Elephant Man* and Brooks helped him deal with orchestrating a large-scale production with its entourage of experienced technicians and actors. The work speaks for itself – a commercial piece of raw cinema that never exploits and never shies away or deviates from Lynch's personal vision. It was even nominated for a number of Oscars.

After *The Elephant Man*, offers for further films flooded in, one of which came from a famous producer with a potentially huge project. Dino de Laurentiis chose Lynch to realise his latest multi-million-dollar picture *Dune*. Based on the much-loved book by Frank Herbert, *Dune* was expected to be box office dynamite so the anticipation and hype were immense. Despite the best efforts of all involved, though, *Dune* was a complete flop. However, part of Lynch's original contract allowed him to make another movie for the de Laurentiis group, with a pay cut in order to obtain complete creative control. The result, *Blue Velvet*, contained many of the themes that would pervade his later work and became an independent hit, highly acclaimed by the critics. It also signalled the moment in Lynch's career where he could work in mainstream cinema yet retain his authorial mark. It was around this time that Lynch became personally involved with Isabella Rossellini, although he didn't recognise her when they first met. 'I was looking at her for a while and when there was a break in the conversation, I said: "Hey, you could be the daughter of Ingrid Bergman." And this other girl said "You idiot she *is* Ingrid Bergman's daughter".[5] Their relationship lasted four years. Lynch's next project was to take him into the world of television. He had formed a creative partnership with Mark Frost, who had worked on the popular 80s police series *Hill Street Blues*. They decided to create a new kind of television series and convinced TV network ABC to produce a pilot based on their ideas. *Twin Peaks* was born and was a huge hit, both in the UK and USA. The hype surrounding it was astonishing with everyone wanting to know 'Who killed Laura Palmer?' But Lynch also wanted to return to the cinema. His friend Monty Montgomery had recently optioned Barry Gifford's novel *Wild at Heart: The Story of Sailor and Lula* and asked if Lynch might want to produce it. Lynch's response was, 'What if I read it, fall in love with it and want to do it myself?'[6] Monty replied that, if that was the case, he could. *Wild at Heart* came at the height of Lynch's public exposure and, despite the mixed reaction received, it won the coveted *Palme d'Or* at the Cannes Film Festival. Meanwhile *Twin Peaks* had been continuing its successful run but eventually ABC declared that the killer's identity had to be revealed. Lynch insisted that he would need to direct that particular episode, which turned out to be the series' most powerful and emotionally charged. After the revelation, however, viewing figures diminished substantially and the network eventually shelved the show. The final episode of the series was greeted with a mixed response from the few die-hard fans who remained loyal throughout. Despite its demise, Lynch managed to return to the world of *Twin Peaks* on the big screen and with a more substantial budget. The film was a prequel to its TV counterpart and followed the last sad and seedy days of Laura Palmer's life. Financed by the French company CiBy2000, this should have marked the first of four films that Lynch would make for the company but only *Fire Walk with Me* and *Lost Highway* were eventually filmed.

Fire Walk with Me failed to set the box office alight and received a critical hammering. Too weird for some, too misogynist for others, it alienated *Twin Peaks'* loyal fan base. 'I think a dark cloud came over me in 1992 and didn't lift until '95.'[7] However, Lynch was involved with a number of smaller projects during this period, including the hilariously absurd TV show *On the Air* which lasted for only a few episodes, the cable television play *Hotel Room* and the remarkable *Lumière et compagnie*. Continuing his deal with CiBy2000 in 1997, Lynch's next feature film *Lost Highway* was 'a psychogenic fugue' which saw him once again team up with writer Barry Gifford. An audacious film which overwhelmed audiences with its uncompromising and resolute vision, *Lost Highway* received a mixed critical reaction at the time but is now rightly lauded as a masterpiece.

After a string of contentious films, both public and critic alike were eager to see how Lynch could shock them further. And shock he did when his intention to film *The Straight Story* was announced – but not in a way that anyone had anticipated. David Lynch was instantly drawn to the story of an old man making a long, slow trip on a lawnmower to reconcile with his dying brother. The film cost less than $10 million and marked the debut feature for Lynch's own production company, The Picture Factory. Perhaps the most surreal aspect of the whole affair was the role of Disney as the film's distributor in the USA. The film was passed as a G, suitable for all and ideal 'family' material.

Mulholland Dr. was originally conceived as a TV series but, despite ABC greenlighting the project and producing a pilot, studio executives grew concerned about the concept and dropped the show. They criticised its pace, violence and weirdness, all elements that had been present in the approved script. Fast forward 18 months and Lynch pulled off a remarkable conjuring trick. He reassembled the cast and crew, developed a conclusion to the pilot, and released *Mulholland Dr.* cinematically. The gamble paid off. *Mulholland Dr.* became a critical success and won (along with the Coen Brothers' *The Man Who Wasn't There*) the Best Director prize at Cannes 2001, Lynch's second major Cannes win. One year later, whilst serving on the jury at Cannes, he was awarded France's highest civil honour, the *Légion d'honneur*.

INLAND EMPIRE marked a new direction for Lynch as he moved away from traditional celluloid filmmaking. 'I started working in DV for my website, and I fell in love with the medium. It's unbelievable, the freedom and the incredible different possibilities it affords, in shooting and in post-production.'[8] *INLAND EMPIRE* premiered at the Venice Film Festival in 2006 where Lynch received the prestigious *Leone d'Oro* (Golden Lion) Award for lifetime achievement.

NOW I'VE SAID MY A,B,C – THE EARLY FILMS

Whilst creating a work for the end of year experimental painting and sculpture contest at the Pennsylvania Academy of the Fine Arts, a chance breeze gave the impression of movement on the apparently static canvas. Immediately Lynch knew what he wanted. 'I wanted to see a painting move and have sound to it.'[9]

Six Figures Getting Sick (1966)

Directed, Produced and Animated by: David Lynch
Crew: Jack Fisk

Six despairing heads confront the viewer, their bodies viewed in negative. From the depths of their exposed innards wells a tide of vomit that bursts forth from their mouths in a torrent of animated colour, covering the lower two-thirds of the screen. The constant wailing of a siren heralds the endless nature of their plight as they try to cover their mouths in vain, only for the whole incident to repeat, announced by a countdown that seals their fate.

With long-time collaborator Jack Fisk, Lynch set about constructing a sculptured screen consisting of a mould of his head onto which a one-minute animated loop would endlessly play to the incessant sound of an air-raid siren. If the lights were sufficiently low the film could be seen distorted through the artist's own features – a hybrid blend of film, sculpture and installation. Elements of this short work would crop up in *The Grandmother* as well as in the staging of *Industrial Symphony No1* with its air-raid dolls. The six heads here are disintegrating, decaying models, their hands cardboard cut-outs.

The mix of media is what makes the whole piece so compelling and disturbing – there is no release from the figures' anguish – and at one point the whole screen turns blood red as the word 'sick' flashes to indicate the next bout of vomited multicoloured paint amidst the monochrome canvas. Stylistically the work recalls the works of Surrealist animators Jan Svankmajer and Walerian Borowczyk in its use of mixed techniques and imperfect objects to create a sense of unease. *Six Figures Getting Sick* bagged Lynch the first prize for his efforts. However, the whole exercise had cost about $200 to make, a vast sum for an impoverished art student, effectively rendering future experimentation in this area impossible without significant outside funding. Fortunately for the young artist another student was interested in the work. H Barton Wasserman approached Lynch and asked him to make a similar film for him.

Armed with a budget of $1,000 and the promise of total directorial control, Lynch purchased a Bolex camera, committing himself to spending many hours figuring out the intricacies of cinematography. The Bolex is one of the mainstays of independent movie making, and animation in particular; its clockwork mechanism and high quality optics make it an ideal first choice for many aspiring cinematographers. Lynch animated the whole film over the next two months. It was an ambitious project involving live action in one-third of the screen and animated segments masked off in the remaining two-thirds. Sadly, though, the end result was not a success for when the film was developed there was nothing but indistinguishable blurs with no frame boundaries. H Barton Wasserman continued to be supportive and let Lynch keep the remaining money to continue with his experiments. Rather than reshoot the painstakingly animated piece, though, he embarked on a new project: *The Alphabet*, a short film comprising live action as well as animation.

The Alphabet (1968)

Directed by: David Lynch
Written by: David Lynch
Produced by: H Barton Wasserman
Edited by: David Lynch
Cinematography: David Lynch
Sound: Robert Cullum, David Lynch, Robert McDonald
Cast: Peggy Lynch (Girl)

'Based on Peggy's niece's nightmare – or rather my imagining of it.'[10]

A young girl lies sleeping in bed, her dreams disturbed by increasingly desperate shouts of 'ABC' by the disembodied voices of children. The alphabet is drawn in front of her from A to Z as the sky extends in pastel shades. A disembodied mouth lulls. A rising seed makes a letter A and gives birth, bleeding, to lower case offspring that form the head of a man. As a sprouting heart from the ejaculation of the man fills its progenitor with letters, the girl awakes screaming as the head disintegrates in a deluge of blood. Covered in spots and pasted with white paint she remembers her alphabet, only to face a similarly bloody fate.

The girl is played by Lynch's wife, Peggy, and the inspiration came from a chance story she related to him. On a family visit Peggy observed her niece having a nightmare, throughout which the young girl was chanting the *Alphabet Song*. This provided the springboard for the film as Lynch tried to imagine what this nightmare must have been like. One can only hope it wasn't quite so deranged.

The Alphabet provides the visual foundations for much of Lynch's later work. One aspect lies in the use of non-contemporaneous make-up. The pasty white make-up associated with the demands of silent cinematography seems to hold a fascination for Lynch and it is a simple way of creating other-worldliness that is genuinely creepy in a modern context.

Fears of siring a deformed child would see their apotheosis in *Eraserhead* and *The Elephant Man*. Indeed the decapitation of Henry in *Eraserhead* is effectively rehearsed in animated form here, albeit with a cubist main figure. What is interesting is that Lynch's influences are quite clear at this stage and they are almost exclusively embedded in the world of traditional arts rather than the moving arts. He has taken the world of Surrealist, Cubist and Naïve painting and given them the extra dimension of time. Unlike many of the Surrealists' own films, Lynch is responding here to the painterly aspects that would be difficult to realise on a live action basis. There are clear nods to Miró, Picasso and Dali in both the composition and visual nature of this film. Even at this early stage the use of sound to create unease and disassociation with the picture shows an understanding of the way vision and sound can be deliberately dissonant or mood provoking. Rushes of air and bass rumbles alternate with disembodied voices to reproduce the girl's dream state.

This was Lynch's first attempt at using sound on film (as opposed to the siren on *Six Figures Getting Sick* which was part of the installation itself) and, despite being crudely recorded, is startling in its effect. Key to the strangeness that permeates the soundtrack was the use of a faulty tape recorder which he used to record the sounds of his baby daughter, Jennifer, crying. The net result of the fault was twofold: first, it produced a deeply disturbing and unsettling background that suitably complemented the on-screen events, but it also meant that Lynch could get back the money he spent hiring the equipment, returned because of the faults.

Despite his enthusiasm Lynch had realised that the whole process of making films was not a cheap one. He was working as a printer in Philadelphia (the same job as Henry in *Eraserhead*) when a recommendation from his friend Bushnell Keeler led him to seek a grant from the American Film Institute. The original script for *The Grandmother* ran to just eight unformed pages and simply described shots or scenes. In some senses a formal script would not be appropriate for such a distinctively unconventional piece. But this script, submitted along with a print of *The Alphabet*, resulted in Lynch being awarded one of the AFI's four annual grants and so *The Grandmother* was born.

The Grandmother (1970)

Directed by: David Lynch
Written by: David Lynch
Produced by: David Lynch
Cinematography: David Lynch
Cast: Richard White (Boy), Dorothy McGinnis (Grandmother), Virginia Maitland (Mother), Robert Chadwick (Father)

Mother and Father have grown from the soil. They crawl around on all fours and make animal noises. They are disturbed by the arrival of Boy and they taunt him aggressively. Boy wets his bed and is punished by Father. Boy has an idea to bring some stability into his life – he will get a Grandmother by planting a seed on a bed, making sure there is adequate soil for her to grow. He tends the plant lovingly as it becomes a fully-fledged pod. He helps his new relative out of her pod and sits her down. Boy and Grandmother have a wonderful time. His parents still treat him cruelly but that can be forgotten. However, all good things come to an end: Grandmother becomes ill and Boy is forced to go to his parents for help. They laugh at him, and his attempts to drag them upstairs are futile. Boy rushes up to see Grandmother, but she is dead.

The basic premise of *The Grandmother,* where a neglected, abused boy creates an imaginary friend, could easily be the basis of any number of TV weepies or moralistic tales of caution and retribution, but not in the hands of David Lynch. Instead the film is a nightmare journey into the psyche of a confused and frightened child, showing the world from the viewpoint of a damaged mind. With his parents reduced to animalistic behaviour, scuttling around, barking or clawing like savage birds it is no wonder that the boy seeks solace with a grandmother. His father is so pent up with anger his face is almost dissected in two; his cackling mother is ineffectual and mean. His parents can hardly mouth a word – instead they bark like dogs. They have become animal-like in their brutality towards the child, either castigating or ignoring him. They treat their own son as one would a dog – rubbing his face in his own waste to discourage him from repeatedly fouling his bed. *The Grandmother* gives us a further vision of a child's nightmare as first explored in *The Alphabet* but here the reason for the boy's nightmare is made apparent to the viewer – his whole waking life is a nightmare to the extent that the barriers between real and dream state on occasion break down completely.

Lynch also shows his love of the Surrealists' use of free-word association as a way of creating images that have a dreamlike reality but also relate to the mind's ability to interpret literally or emotionally rather than figuratively. In the Buñuel/Dali film *Un Chien Andalou* (1929) the main protagonist gets his hand caught in a shutting door. Ants start pouring from the hole that has appeared in his hand – a literal interpretation of 'fourmis dans la main', an expression meaning 'pins and needles' in English. In *The Grandmother* Lynch employs similar word associations. The young boy literally soils his sheets but associates this with actual soil in which he grows his grandmother. Lynch also uses visual and aural association to emphasise aspects of this bizarre world. The boy's urine-soaked sheets make a large orange circle that becomes associated with the sun, which is also necessary to grow the seed.

If the odd events were not enough to create a sense of unease, Lynch uses a formidable arsenal of cinematic techniques both to distance the viewer and disorientate them. First there are extended animated sequences depicting the growth of the family from the seed and their eventual execution in the mind of the boy. These are a combination of photo-montage, paints and mixed media of a similar style to that used in *The Alphabet,* but here they are more integrated in the film's disjointed but linear narrative. Both films use primitive drawings to reflect the child's view of the world and create a further sense of distancing from the adult (more conscious) mind. In contrast the use of animation in *Eraserhead* is fully realised and professional: Henry's mind has passed the boundaries of childish imagination and ascended into adulthood.

Then there's the use of altering set space: the boy's bedroom alters throughout the film to create different states of mind, sometimes just a bed and a chest of drawers against the stark black backdrop showing isolation in the void. More startling still is the use of pixillation for some, but not all, of the characters' movements (and not necessarily scenes that would traditionally require animating), which makes the actions appear stilted, jittery and unnatural. The effect of disassociation is enhanced by the contrast with conventional live-action shots. Sometimes the jump from real to pixillated image is used in a single perceived shot to startling effect. Then there is the make-up, which, like in *The Alphabet,* is deliberately pasty and reminiscent of silent film star make-up gone wrong, caked and improperly applied. This accentuates any colour in a frame, be it the red around the eyes or an open screaming mouth. Along with the use of monochromatic sets the film at times appears almost black and white, so these splashes of colour provide focal points in the otherwise bleached-out world.

The Grandmother continues the theme of decapitation or headshot death that runs through much of Lynch's work. Often this is used to indicate some castration complex, most notably in *Eraserhead*, but here it is purely wish fulfilment as the boy imagines his parents' death in a makeshift theatre, an animated Grand Guignol to placate the boy's frustration at his plight. These flights of fancy externalise in the figure of the grandmother herself. The boy's world is so polluted by his experiences that even she seems sinister, and her smile and plump demeanour do little to dispel the dead look in her eyes. He has grown his grandmother on a bed in a pile of soil from a bag of seeds, tended lovingly between beatings from his father. This, of course, runs counter to our commonly accepted notions of what a grandmother is: by definition a biological grandmother is born *before* her grandson. It could be interpreted that the grandmother is really there, that the boy has dug her from the cemetary beside their house, his interpretation of birth being analogous to that of plants emerging from soil.

The grandmother is also incapable of proper speech: no one in the film can do more than mouth words or bark out indecipherable sounds, and she whistles like a boiling kettle as the last vestiges of life exit her body, a human balloon deflating in front of the helpless lad. The last hope of any love in his life has faded away, and the grandmother who kissed him and was there to hold him has breathed her last. All attempts to rouse his parents to her aid are futile. They don't care or even believe in the grandmother.

This film is a true oddity but contains many of the themes and ideas of Lynch's later work, and shows a remarkable grasp of the medium. At just over 30 minutes, *The Grandmother* falls into that twilight category of film that is too short to be a feature and too long to be a short film. It is a baptism of fire to those unfamiliar with Lynch's work.

HI YA SONNY, WHAT'VE YOU GOT THERE?

By 1970 Lynch had decided that filmmaking was what he wanted to do. He had been offered a scholarship at the American Film Institute Center for Advanced Film Studies but after a year the young student was becoming agitated with some aspects of the course and decided to quit. In order to keep him on board the AFI offered him a deal he couldn't refuse... the chance to make *Eraserhead*. They had seen the script for the film and allowed the vast premises of the school to be used to mount the production – there are some exteriors but for the most part this is a distinctly studio-bound film – so Lynch managed to obtain the college's disused stables, even treating them as a home for much of the shoot. A budget was agreed.

Unfortunately the AFI didn't realise the scale and ambition of the venture. Lynch's screenplay was 21 pages. In normal film production there is a page to length ratio – one page equals roughly one minute of screen time. The AFI thought, despite Lynch's indications to the contrary, that the film would be 21 minutes long. Production was to start in 1971 following auditions for all the main roles but the film would not be completed for many years. Lynch's meticulous attention to detail and the set construction took up much of the time but the real enemy was money. When the initial funds dried up production was halted after a year. Every time another source of funding dripped in, production resumed. For example, in one scene Henry enters his room. An entire year passed between the shots of him opening the door and actually entering. For a large part of this time poor Jack Nance was stuck with a goofy hair-do. 'Jack was such a professional, I can tell you!' Lynch has commented.[11] When eventually the film was completed, thanks in part to additional funding from Sissy Spacek and Jack Fisk, who had regularly handed Lynch paycheques, over half a decade had passed.

The Amputee (1974)

Directed by: David Lynch
Produced by: David Lynch
Cinematography: Frederick Elmes
Cast: Catherine E Coulson (Woman), David Lynch (Doctor)

An amputee sits in her chair writing her memoirs on a pad of paper, casually puffing at a cigarette in bitter nostalgic recollection. A doctor enters and treats the stump of her left leg, which is weeping profusely. Then, wordlessly, he leaves.

Produced quickly during a hiatus in the filming of *Eraserhead* about a year into its arduous creation, *The Amputee* is not one short but two.

Asked to test two different kinds of videotape stock for possible bulk purchase by the AFI, cinematographer Frederick Elmes' original intention was to shoot a couple of pieces of graduated card, as is standard practice, to determine the better of the two. Lynch convinced him that they might as well make a short film, shoot it twice and test the stock, taking advantage of the opportunity. The result was *The Amputee* with future Log Lady and *Eraserhead* technician Catherine Coulson as the titular character. In the film Lynch, starring as the Doctor, comes in and washes her stumps. The whole event is played out in a single static take with the amputee herself seemingly oblivious to the attentions of the doctor, lost in thought about relationships past. The overall look of the film shows why Lynch was concerned at the time about the American Film Institute suddenly being interested in adopting video stock. With video still being very much in its infancy at the time, the effect is muddied and distorted but not in the organic way of, say, 8mm film. There are plentiful smudges and rolling, stretched segments; the contrast is ill-defined.

The sound in *The Amputee* consists of diegetic effects overlaid with a monologue of the amputee's internal thoughts. The gurgling noise of the leaking limb is quite revolting and sounds like many of the foley effects on *Eraserhead*, albeit tinnier. Of some curiosity value, it is around this time that Lynch told Coulson that he could see her starring in a television show holding a log, predating *Twin Peaks* by almost twenty years. The show – to be called *I Test My Log with Every Branch of Knowledge* – would feature Coulson as a widow who uses her log to find out facts about certain subjects such as dentistry. The result would have been an absurdist documentary, informative and yet surreal. Instead it would be many years before the much-loved Log Lady would make her screen debut.

Eraserhead (1977)

Directed by: David Lynch
Written by: David Lynch
Produced by: David Lynch
Edited by: David Lynch
Cinematography: Herbert Cardwell & Frederick Elmes
Cast: Jack Nance (Henry Spencer), Charlotte Stewart (Mary X), Allen Joseph (Mr X), Jeanne Bates (Mrs X), Judith Anna Roberts (Beautiful Girl Across the Hall), Laurel Near (Lady in the Radiator), Jack Fisk (Man in the Planet), Jean Lange (Grandmother), Brad Keeler (Little Boy), Toby Keeler (Man Fighting), Jennifer Lynch (Little Girl)

The Man in the Planet releases a sperm into the world below. The permanently confused Henry stumbles through an industrial wasteland to his apartment. He learns that his girlfriend Mary X has invited him round to dinner at her parents' house. There he is served a bizarre meal and then confronted by Mrs X, who asks whether he has had sexual relations with Mary. She goes on to explain that they have a child, and the couple must marry and look after it.

Back at Henry's house, the baby is just an amphibious head and a round, bandaged stomach. Mary becomes frustrated with its constant crying and returns to her parents leaving Henry alone with it. It appears to be in distress. Next morning the baby is covered with spots and very sick. The Beautiful Girl Across the Hall invites herself in and seduces Henry.

The Lady in the Radiator dances across her stage and when the music stops, she crushes Henry's sperm with her foot. Henry stumbles onto the stage. He moves behind a stand as if in court and anxiously twists the rail. Suddenly his head pops off, rolls out of the window and falls to the wasteground below. A young kid picks it up and takes it to a factory where it is made into pencil top rubbers.

Henry returns to the baby. Curiosity leads him to cut away the bandages around its body. To his horror, he finds he has cut the baby right open and it is simply a mass of bleeding, pulsating organs. Henry drives some scissors deep into the mewling child. The Man in the Planet looks on. Henry finds the Lady in the Radiator and they embrace.

Eraserhead became the cult movie that launched Lynch onto an unsuspecting world. A dark, bizarre universe of strange creatures and pervasive sexuality, it tapped into a marketplace that was beginning to come to terms with the rise of the vacuous blockbuster as the sole viewable entertainment. Despite its exemplary production values, *Eraserhead* was the antithesis of the Hollywood product: filmed in black and white rather than glorious Technicolor, elliptic as opposed to explanatory, and challenging rather than disposable. Thirty years on and it still has lost none of its power while many of its contemporaries have slouched into obscurity or retro-kitsch. However odd, *Eraserhead* has an internally consistent, perfectly realised world. Its oddness – the Man in the Planet, the eraser-making machine, the mini-chickens – is not explained away by simple narrative asides or cinematic signposting, it's simply there for the audience to accept. This world is so insular that it exists apart from anything in our everyday life even as it reflects it. In many ways this is much more of a science fiction film than *Star Wars* (1977) ever was – taking us to a galaxy far, far away yet closer to home. The use of black and white cinematography, the soundtrack of menacing rumbles and industrial sounds mixed with a pipe organ all collude to make a sensory experience that is utterly otherworldly.

Eraserhead is about one man's inability to adapt to his environment – a fish out of water. It's tempting to view Henry as an exaggerated substitute for Lynch himself. Having come from the quiet state of Montana the jolt at being confronted by the urban chaos of Philadelphia had a profound effect on the young artist. The petty street violence, the industrial wastelands of factories and skeletal shells of failed industrialism made for a kind of Boschian cityscape of oppression. It is symptomatic of Lynch's work that industrial growth is viewed with abject horror yet at the same time with fascination, for its textures, decay and clutter. Henry is overwhelmed by this environment, to the extent that much of the film takes place inside his room/womb where he feels some modicum of safety. Of course this turns out not to be the case as his world becomes increasingly defined by his claustrophobic surroundings. Henry spirals into a madness brought about by his environment and the invading of his space by his child. His room is his refuge – everyone else who enters it creates additional confusion for the fragile-minded printer. All of them leave – Mary and his neighbour – all save his own progeny. It proves to be his undoing.

Henry's entire predicament has come about through sex. His waking and sleeping fantasies (if, indeed, you view them as fantasies and not portals into other worlds) are all of a twisted sexual nature. He is petrified of sex and its consequences as much as he desires it. The consequences are all too apparent – the Man in the Planet has released the single spermatozoon that fertilises Mary's egg, the result being a severely premature baby, if indeed it is human at all. The baby becomes a constant reminder of the results of Henry's sexual activity, and the results aren't pretty. He sees the way that sex has crippled him via the other denizens that populate his world: the giggling, coy Lady in the Radiator seems to offer the wholesome 'girl next door' attraction with her simple dress and shy cupped hands, but in fact she becomes an aggressor, squishing Henry's sperm under her tiny feet while engaging him directly with her gaze. His own obsession with the downside of sexual activity is mirrored in his fearful dream that indicates a castration complex. Standing on trial his head is ripped from his body by a penis jutting from his neck only for this to be replaced by the wailing head of his own child. Henry can't control his basic sexual urges even if he takes a passive role in them. He tries to engage in sex with Mary but she brushes him away. Later on he has sex with the Beautiful Girl Across the Hall, sinking in a pool of liquid that is a product of their lust as they melt into the bed. Both events, unsuccessful and successful, are watched over by the child, a reminder of the potential consequences.

Henry is passive almost to the point of inactivity. His inability to have any influence on his own destiny and his inherent fatalism makes him a bizarre precursor to the *Angriest Dog in the World*. Henry allows life to happen to him; he is scared of everything and never takes the initiative. Everything – his fling with his neighbour, his acceptance of marriage, even carving a chicken – is done at the instigation of others. He can't even bring himself to stop the advances of his future mother-in-law despite his girlfriend Mary being present. 'I'm too nervous,' is his only defence. He doesn't go to visit Mary or even try to find out whether he is still going out with her. 'I didn't know if you wanted me to come or not.' Henry rarely stands up for himself in any fashion. When he argues with Mary it takes him an age to muster a single derogatory comment before he shies away into his own insecurity. This turmoil is constantly building up inside him but the tension cannot remain unspent. When Henry does finally make a decision in his life it's a monumental one – infanticide.

Henry is, for the most part, like a deadpan silent comedian, a bedraggled Buster Keaton in ill-fitting trousers, walking awkwardly through the industrial wastelands nervously clutching his bag of shopping. This is the comedy of doomed inevitability. The soundtrack plays organ music of the type associated with old cinemas, further enhancing the feeling that Henry is a comedy actor in a world that will treat him harshly. He is given the task of carving the poussin 'just like a regular chicken' at Mary's parents' house and shows a stoical sense of inevitability as the cooked bird billows out blood and starts twitching under his blade. Despite the complete absurdity of the event, Henry seems resigned to the fact that this sort of thing happens to him all the time. When Mary leaves him because the baby is keeping her awake we are treated to the bizarre sight of her at the bottom of Henry's bed, jerking uncontrollably. Henry looks on with his usual resignation: perhaps Mary is having a fit. When it is revealed that all she is trying to do is retrieve her suitcase from under the bed we realise that this is another moment of the absurd as part of the mundane. It's merely our perspective that has created confusion as to its meaning. For Lynch the meaning is there in the comic and emotional feeling of the situation, not the event itself.

Crackles of electricity invade Henry's sanctuary. Electricity is a chaotic force that flows through Lynch's films. It is ubiquitous and a portent for unease or intervention from another plane. Electricity alters the lighting of a room. It is the unsung necessity behind modern life. Lynch brings electricity to the surface by showing its effects through flickering bulbs, arcing wires, the instability of an inadequately wired circuit. It's also signalled by its buzzing sound. A recurring image is that of striped zigzag floors that represent a visualisation of electricity all around us – the very floors that make up the lobby in Henry's apartment block or the rooms of the Black Lodge in *Twin Peaks*. In the original cut of the film electricity played an even greater role – for one scene two girls (one played by Catherine Coulson) were to be tied to a bed while being menaced by a guy with a car battery and cabling. It was just one of many scenes that didn't make it into the final film. Another had Catherine Coulson as the nurse who hands over Henry and Mary's child, and another further featured a bemused Henry tugging at a dead cat. The cat in question was covered in tar, put there by Lynch following an autopsy he had conducted on the animal to see the beauty of its insides.

You have to wonder at Henry's choice of girlfriend when looking at her family. The X's are bizarre by any standards: the wide-eyed father is an enthusiastic madman with a dead arm. Mother bursts into fits at the table, forces Henry to marry her daughter and tries to molest him. Grandmother is virtually comatose but does enjoy the odd cigarette as she tosses the salad – aided and abetted by Mrs X of course. It's no wonder that Mary is strange and that their offspring, premature or otherwise, bears little resemblance to anything we would recognise as a human baby. That said, the infant does have characteristics that make it more 'real' than many of the actual people that populate this strange world. Its needs are simple but constant and understandable – it appears odd but its wants are primitive and all too human. Looking like a fleshy ET, it gurgles, splutters and wheezes its way to an untimely and tragic demise. We have already seen that Henry is capable of violence against his offspring: having taken a leaf from the Lady in the Radiator's book he has hurled the sperm-like progenitors of these mutant children against his wall, trying to wrest his seed from his sleeping girlfriend. Ultimately he kills the child, removing its bandages to reveal that it has no outside, only internal organs. He stabs the screaming creature to put it out of its misery and is engulfed in its porridge-like emissions. Henry's reward for actually doing something is death, but a death which has enlightenment in the white glow of the afterlife. Joining the Lady in the Radiator he discovers that, yes, in heaven everything is fine.

Shot in black and white, Herb Cardwell was the original cinematographer. Leaving for financial reasons, he was replaced by Fred Elmes. It is a testament to the dedication of all involved that the final image on the screen is so consistent. Alan Splet's sound is astonishingly good for a debut feature. It comprises a tableau of noises and establishes the atmosphere of the film, but not only in a sinister or disturbing way. Indeed, the trial scene is lightened by the noise of Henry's penis-enhanced decapitation, a springy cartoon 'boing'. The effects are also innovative and the baby in particular is a masterpiece of modelling. It acts in the most realistic manner, complete with slowly rolling eyeballs and puckered-up mouth that awaits food then spits it out. Lynch has never explained how the model, nicknamed 'Spike' by Jack Nance, was made and worked, and, in this age of CGI where everybody knows how special effects are created, it seems entirely appropriate to retain this mystery.

LIFE IS FULL OF SURPRISES

At first glance the thought of an all-American Surrealist, trendy amongst the midnight movie crowd for his disturbing and impenetrable existential horror film, fronting a British Victorian costume drama must have seemed like box office suicide. A cast of well-respected actors of the stage and screen, including a knight of the realm, and location filming far from home in an alien British society must have seemed a daunting prospect for the young director. Look a little closer, though, and it all becomes clear. *The Elephant Man*, whatever its comments on class and its recourse to annunciating stage dialogue, is quintessentially Lynch on almost every level.

The Elephant Man (1980)

Directed by: David Lynch
Written by: Eric Bergren, Christopher De Vore, David Lynch
Produced by: Jonathan Sanger, Stuart Cornfeld (exec)
Edited by: Anne V Coates
Cinematography: Freddie Francis
Cast: Anthony Hopkins (Dr Frederick Treves), John Hurt (John Merrick), Anne Bancroft (Mrs Kendal), John Gielgud (Carr Gomm), Wendy Hiller (Mrs Mothershead), Freddie Jones (Bytes), Michael Elphick (Night Porter), Hannah Gordon (Mrs Treves), Dexter Fletcher (Bytes' Boy), Lesley Dunlop (Nora)

'This exhibit degrades all who see it, as well as the poor creature himself.'

In Victorian England, Dr Frederick Treves wanders through an urban carnival in search of freak shows. He happens upon a creature called the Elephant Man and pays the owner, Mr Bytes, to allow an examination. His purpose is to present a paper to the Pathological Society and enhance his medical reputation. The Elephant Man is returned to Bytes but is savagely beaten and suffering from bronchitis, so Treves admits him to the hospital. In an attempt to convince the authorities to allow the man to stay, Treves endeavours to communicate with him. He discovers that he can talk and is educated. His name is John Merrick. He is given rooms and settles in comfortably, gradually becoming accepted by most members of staff. One of the night porters, however, sees a money-spinner and each evening gathers together a drunken crowd of people who will pay to see the freak.

Treves attempts to introduce Merrick to London society and the newspapers run articles about him. Actress Mrs Kendal visits him with tales of the theatre and gives him a photograph of herself and a copy of Shakespeare's plays. Merrick becomes a fixture on the social circuit and is visited by many local bigwigs, who barely disguise their disgust at his appearance.

However, the night porter is still in business. One evening, Bytes joins the throng and, after a particularly humiliating brawl, kidnaps Merrick and takes him to France. Severely neglected, he is once more put on show. However, Bytes' boy can no longer stand the abuse and, with the other circus freaks, releases Merrick and assists his escape back to England. Reunited with Treves, it appears that Merrick does not have long to live. He visits the theatre to see a production of *Puss in Boots*, and Mrs Kendal dedicates the performance to him. Back at the hospital, Merrick thanks his friend Dr Treves for a splendid evening and discards all the pillows from his bed, determined to lie down to sleep like everybody else. He sleeps one final time, his mother welcoming him to the bright glory of heaven.

In the battle between what is right and what feels right Lynch always plumps for the latter. His films are not about objective or subjective truth, but emotional truth. A film may well tag itself as 'a true story about courage and dignity' but, like any biopic that forefronts its true life credentials, the actuality, by necessity, is often far removed. A number of the characters portrayed in the film did exist but many of the events are fabricated. The real Elephant Man, actually named Joseph Merrick, did not, aside from his deformities, suffer any other illness. Nor was he mistreated. He even approached a showman in the industry in order to earn a reasonable income as a showpiece. This wasn't a concern for Lynch, however, who wanted to show an emotionally correct *idea* of John Merrick rather than a factual one. And in doing so he affords us an opportunity to reach the essence of the man as representation.

It is difficult to make a film about exploitation without inviting criticisms of exploitation. *The Elephant Man* initially signposts itself as a horror picture but metamorphoses into a drama about Merrick's humanity. The audience members are therefore forced to confront their own curiosity and ability to dehumanise their fellow man. They are then faced with their insensitivity and the true horror, which is Merrick's situation as an intelligent being rather than an insensitive novelty.

The film opens with screams of distress as Merrick's mother is trampled by elephants in an apocryphal prologue, which turn to screams of delight as we see the fairground that houses Merrick amongst its many exhibits. The contrast between screams of terror and joy is what makes up Merrick's life: he is either a figure of disgust or a source of ridicule, often both. As we follow Frederick Treves into the shadows on his search for medical curiosities it becomes apparent that the main exhibit is indescribable even for hardened patrons of the carnival. The camera tracking is deliberately slow paced. We see only glimpses of the hideous apparition but the look in Treves' eyes says it all. Coupled with the orders barked by owner Bytes' boy and the beatings delivered by Bytes himself, the signs are there – this is a monster.

Even the language used to describe Merrick by all those around him is bestial and degrading; he is a wretch, 'twisted and perverted', Bytes' 'creature', 'the greatest freak in the world'. In traditional horror films this uneducated mute would escape his shackles and go on a rampage. The maid who screams at his hideous appearance (in a 'plate of food dropping' moment mirroring many a Hammer film) would be simply another victim. But, as we soon learn, this is not a horror film in the traditional sense, but an emotional one, and the knowledge of Merrick's humanity allows the film to segue from exploitation into drama. Although the character of Merrick remains exploited throughout the entire running time, it's not by the film. The key turning point is voiced by Treves: 'The man's a complete idiot. I pray to God he's an idiot.' The awfulness of Merrick's plight would be much easier to bear if he was unaware of it. But his humanity is his greatest tormentor. And ultimately it's his humanity that becomes his salvation.

More than any other film in Lynch's oeuvre *The Elephant Man* is concerned with the act of staging and watching. Theatre and its artifice hold sway in most of his films, from the Lady in the Radiator and the Silencio Club to the filmmaking sub-plots of *Mulholland Dr.* and *INLAND EMPIRE*, but *The Elephant Man* takes the notion to extremes: almost everyone is involved in some way with staging, showing and artificiality. All the characters are voyeurs, although Merrick only becomes one towards the end of the film as he finally sees the joys of the theatre first hand. Bytes puts Merrick on show and people gawp at his monstrous body, the essence of any freak show. Treves attempts to distance himself from such barbarity but happily exhibits Merrick to the medical college, where he is paraded before the students, pointed at with sticks and ultimately stripped of all clothes along with the last vestiges of his dignity. Throughout, Treves talks about him as if he isn't present or aware, commenting on his genitals in a society that, on the surface, viewed any sexual reference as immoral. The curtains that shield Merrick's modesty in silhouette from the viewer are but a false veil of respectability; such niceties do not take place in Merrick's world outside.

It takes Treves some while to realise his own hypocrisy: 'I'm beginning to believe that me and Mr Bytes are rather alike.' His aims are to further his medical career and ultimately his bank balance. His accusation to Bytes that 'all you do is profit from another person's misery' can just as aptly be applied to him. When Merrick later becomes a celebrity he is still on stage, either as a society plaything for the rich – 'they only want to impress their friends' – or through the evening assaults by the night porter and his paying entourage of drunks and whores. That his first patron should be the 'facile' society theatre actress Mrs Kendal further stretches this link. When he finally sees a pantomime of *Puss in Boots* he is once more made a spectacle for the furtherance of the audience's hypocritical need for belief in their own Christian worthiness. He can finally watch someone else on stage but, as Mrs Kendal dedicates the performance to him, he once again becomes the object of the gaze.

It is no accident that Mrs Kendal's first present to Merrick is a picture of herself. Apart from the narcissism of the act – she deems it a more important gift than the writings of Shakespeare – it is another example of watching. Merrick's only other possession is a far smaller framed photograph of his mother, which triggers memories of her and terrible dreams. In Lynch's world the photograph, framed, is often of significance. In *The Elephant Man* Merrick is fascinated by the multitude of framed photographs that clutter the mantelpiece over Treves' fireplace. A similar montage can be seen in the Palmer's house a hundred years and thousands of miles away. The final shot in most episodes of *Twin Peaks* was of a framed picture of Laura Palmer and here the photograph

of Merrick's mother bookends the film. Pictures on the walls, too, have significance in *Fire Walk With Me* and *Mulholland Dr.* In *The Elephant Man* they represent a longing for something Merrick can never have more than once, a normal night's sleep, perchance to dream.

The Elephant Man also succeeds in depicting Victorian England at the moment of rapid industrialisation, of a sort the world had not witnessed before. Lynch's use of the industrial signifies both progress and fear. It invades the space even when unseen. In the opening hallucinatory explanation of Merrick's birth, when his pregnant mother is crushed by marching elephants, the sounds that accompany her slowed agonised screams are those of rhythmic pounding machinery, representational of the elephants but also the relentless, often destructive, march of industrialism. Industry fills in the corners of *The Elephant Man* with its heaps of coal, men pounding lathes, spewing chimneys and smoke-billowing factories. When we first see Treves at work he is treating the injuries of an industrial accident: 'Abominable things these machines. You can't reason with them.' It's a theme that runs throughout Lynch's work, a pull between inevitable progress, a fascination with the machine, and a yearning for a perceived better life of rural simplicity. In this respect the environment of *The Elephant Man* resembles the industrial hell of *Eraserhead*'s virtual Philadelphia.

Rather like Tod Browning's notorious *Freaks* (1932), *The Elephant Man* is not about sympathising with its subject but empathising with it. Sympathy evokes feelings of pity or detachment. Both Browning and Lynch's films attempt to let the other in, to become, if you will, 'one of us', even if society at large cannot allow it. That which is perceived as monstrous can be a force for good or ill, or is often just ambivalent. These characters are defined by much more than their ailment or disability, depicted with a rare humanity.

The film's closing moments show Merrick's mother floating in the night as he sleeps properly for the only time in his life. In heaven everything is fine. The delicate way that Merrick passes from this world appears at odds with the David Lynch that many regard as sadistic and gratuitous. Yet often his characters do receive a better hereafter. There is hope that something good will survive the horrors and unfairness of the everyday. And if there is a hope in John Merrick's plight it is in his assertion that 'I am happy every hour of the day... because I am loved'. The power of love in all of Lynch's work is very much related to Buddhist consciousness – the way of Albert Rosenfield – that paves a way for a better and peaceful existence. It is also a love, however, which recognises that pain, struggle and heartache are intrinsic to the human condition. The way to enlightenment is to transcend the misery of the real world to realise a higher existence. Curiously the final shot leads almost directly to the opening of Lynch's next film, the altogether more bombastic *Dune*.

THE WEIRDING WAY

Frank Herbert's quasi-mystical science fiction epic *Dune* was never going to be easy to adapt for the cinema. Optioned in 1972, the first major stab at reproducing the doorstep-sized novel was undertaken by maverick Surrealist director Alejandro Jodorowsky, a tempting prospect if ever there was one. Despite millions being spent on pre-production the film was ultimately shelved. The option lapsed and was snapped up by Dino de Laurentiis on the advice of his daughter Raffaella. Ridley Scott, hot off *Alien*, was initially approached to direct, with production design to be handled by HR Giger; but again the project fell through. A viewing of *The Elephant Man* led the producers to approach Lynch, which is not as strange as it may at first seem. Dino de Laurentiis had previously produced a number of science fiction films, which had imaginative choices for director (Mike Hodges' *Flash Gordon* [1980] and Roger Vadim's *Barbarella* [1967]). It was unusual, though, that he granted the young director such a huge budget – around $40 million, a massive amount at the time, making it one of the most expensive films ever made – also allowing him to develop the script, the very stumbling block that had caused previous attempts to falter. Lynch was to turn in eight drafts of the script before he was happy with the results.

Dune (1984)

Directed by: David Lynch
Written by: David Lynch from the novel by Frank Herbert
Produced by: Dino de Laurentiis & Raffaella de Laurentiis
Edited by: Antony Gibbs
Cinematography: Freddie Francis
Cast: Francesca Annis (Lady Jessica), Leonardo Cimino (The Baron's Doctor), Brad Dourif (Piter De Vries), José Ferrer (Padishah Emperor Shaddam IV), Linda Hunt (Shadout Mapes), Freddie Jones (Thufir Hawat), Richard Jordan (Duncan Idaho), Kyle MacLachlan (Paul Atreides), Virginia Madsen (Princess Irulan), Silvana Mangano (Reverend Mother Ramallo), Everett McGill (Stilgar), Kenneth McMillan (Baron Vladimir Harkonnen), Jack Nance (Nefud), Siân Phillips (Reverend Mother Gaius Helen Mohiam), Jürgen Prochnow (Duke Leto Atreides), Paul Smith (The Beast Rabban), Patrick Stewart (Gurney Halleck), Sting (Feyd-Rautha), Dean Stockwell (Doctor Wellington Yueh), Max von Sydow (Doctor Kynes), Alicia Witt (Alia), Sean Young (Chani), David Lynch (Spice Worker)

The universe is dominated by the presence of the spice Melange which extends life, expands consciousness and can fold space, allowing interstellar travel. It exists in one place, the desert planet Arrakis, also known as Dune. The Emperor of the known universe is concerned that House Atreides of the planet Caladan is becoming too powerful and plots with its enemies, House Harkonnen, to allow the Atreides to guard Dune before ambushing them. Paul Atreides, the Duke's son, cannot understand why the Harkonnen would give up their presence on Arrakis, but understands the family must go nonetheless. His mother Jessica is a Bene Gesserit, of a secret order of women, regarded by some as witches. Their Reverend Mother tests Paul by exposing him to horrific pain. She tells him of the Water of Life, bile from the Arrakis worms, which no man has ever drunk and survived. Only the Kwisatz Haderach, the true Messiah, can drink it.

On Geidi Prime the mad Baron Harkonnen plans to invade Arrakis and coerces Dr Yueh, servant of Duke Atreides, to attack the Duke. Yueh agrees to spare the lives of Jessica and Paul if the Duke breathes poison gas into the face of the Baron. The Duke agrees but fails in his mission. Jessica and Paul are taken to the desert to be abandoned, but escape their captors. They reach the mountains and find sanctuary with the Fremen, the inhabitants of Dune who have a legend that tells of the coming of a Messiah from another world. Jessica drinks the Water of Life and becomes the new Reverend Mother; as a result her daughter Alia is born prematurely but possessing great power. She and Paul (now Maud'Dib) teach the Fremen to fight, beginning a war to stop the flow of spice and halt intergalactic travel. Paul drinks the Water of Life and leads the Fremen to launch an attack on the Harkonnen. The Emperor travels to Dune to find out from the Baron why the spice is no longer flowing. Alia kills the Baron and Paul finally confronts the Emperor. As the storm clouds build up it begins to rain on Arrakis.

Adapting close on 600 pages of book to screen with faithful accuracy was never going to be possible without an unlimited budget and a 24-hour running time. Lynch's screenplay tries to condense as much of the novel as possible into a film just shy of two and a half hours. There are details in the asides and background that hint at a wider picture but these are only for people familiar with the book. The result is one of the most dense science fiction films ever made with little space for introspection and a bewildering array of alien names and places to take in. To be fair, this constant alien-ness is present in *Star Wars* (1977), a film that takes the themes of *Dune*, its ideas of Jihad, rebellion and mysticism, and covers them in candyfloss. The difference in *Star Wars* is that these details are analogous to verbal art design; there to provide texture. In *Dune* they are integral to the narrative and necessary to understanding the film itself. In order to give some sense of direction to the proceedings – tittle-tattle, backstabbing and intergalactic diplomacy – the screenplay focuses upon Paul Atreides as the spiritual heart of the film. Played by Kyle MacLachlan, a young actor making his screen debut, he has said, 'I couldn't believe I got the role. I don't know any character I feel closer to.'[12] For a number of years, MacLachlan would become the quintessential male lead for Lynch.

Dune is less a film about big battles, spaceships and giant monsters than it is about the awakening of consciousness and a journey to enlightenment. This was the very theme of the book (emptiness, awakening, development, rebellion) that made it a success in the late 1960s. Lynch embellishes this by foregrounding the ideas of dreamspace as necessary to spiritual furtherance. Dreams provide the extra-material road that Paul Atreides must walk down; the spice that enables interstellar travel through the folding of space also develops accelerated consciousness in him. As the links between the spice, the worms, the folding of space and the hallucinatory visions all converge, Paul's messianic role becomes apparent as he ascends towards apotheosis. Through violence Paul can obtain universal peace; the contradiction of pain, suffering and violence leading to pacifism. His actual existence is irrelevant but the idea of his existence is enough to create a change: he has become the word and the word is power and revolution.

The visions point to Paul's emergence as the Messiah but their purpose in the context of the film lies also in their link to the conscious state and the visualisation of the hallucinatory shamanistic effects of the spice. Although Paul is the focus of the film's dreams (indeed the whole film could be seen as a dream) it is the Guild Navigators, those huge, floating, fleshy orifices that fold space, who demonstrate the spice's physical properties. The act of folding space to allow intergalactic travel is not portrayed as a technical one but a spiritual one brought about by the spice's ability to alter the user's consciousness and become one with the universe. It is 'travelling without moving' – transcendental travel. Ultimately this is why Paul Maud'Dib wishes to halt spice production, because it is a drug fix to simple enlightenment that would ultimately throw the delicate nature of the universe off balance. It is appropriate, therefore, that his house is one more readily associated with the organic and natural, its wood interiors like some futuristic Great

Northern Hotel. Even the threats to assassinate Paul are naturalistic. The fact that in an age of space travel the House Atreides still favours the knife over the gun (force shields notwithstanding) indicates why the Bene Gesserit sisterhood should find the Messiah there.

Paul Atreides provides the film with its spiritual and narrative drive, but it is Baron Vladimir Harkonnen that creates the most lasting impression. A rotund and insane experimenter of deranged cruelty, the Baron is one of Lynch's most grotesque creations and allows for moments of perverse breathing space punctuating Paul's story. Lingering on the deformed body as textural art is a technique Lynch often employs. Here, though, the monstrous exterior reflects the monstrous interior, as opposed, say, to John Merrick whose external countenance belies his inner gentleness and dignity. There is also plenty of opportunity for Lynch to show grotesque spectacle reduced to the routinely mundane. When the Baron is having his erupting boils tended to, one of the surgeons directs, 'Put the pick in there, Pete, and turn it round real slow'. It's a moment that is professional, bizarre and utterly disgusting. Clearly then, against all the splendour and pomp of the other houses, it's the Harkonnen that have the most fun. The Baron operates on a helpless waif of a captive, much like Lynch himself did on a dead cat during the making of *Eraserhead*. Indeed the Baron enjoys the company of animals: a cat and mouse are tied together to provide him with some bizarre cure/catalyst for his sickness. He relishes debasing life: having captured Jessica, he enjoys 'just some spittle in your face' before specifying dark sexual desires. The Baron is an ego unrestrained; he floats around oozing puss and barking 'give me spice' unhindered by social convention. Geidi Prime, the Harkonnen homeworld with its heterogeneous collection of factories and smoke-billowing industrial plant, contrasts directly with the ordered, regal world of Caladan. Geidi Prime is another example of the fear and beauty contrast in the multifarious world of rampant industrialisation. The Baron revels in being covered in industrial oil and technological gadgetry, in using machinery to demean life.

The link between sound and action is always at the heart of Lynch's films and often the use of sound counterpoints the action. Although *Dune* is no exception it does differ in that sound implicitly affects the action. This is a world where words and sound can kill, where the mentioning of an idea can alter the future. The very utterance of 'Maud'Dib' is enough to destroy in the hands of Paul's Freman army.

The science fiction genre often appeals to the sense of spectacle as part of its remit: to view fantastic things, to see the impossible. It is therefore difficult to distance the genre from the special effects work that makes it possible. Indeed, in some senses, effects are what characterises cinema as an art form unlike any other; the illusion of reality is its greatest achievement. Much of Lynch's work relies on effects but normally to create a mood, and usually in a way that reflects his empathy with the early Surrealist filmmakers. He even went so far as to create test make-up for *The Elephant Man* before contracting Christopher Tucker to do the job. What is impressive about these hands-on effects, such as the baby in *Eraserhead*, is how little they have dated. In *Dune* a vast array of effects shots were called for, requiring a number of differing techniques. The simplest ones are amongst the best, for example, the floating syringe that threatens to assassinate Paul. For the most part the pre-CGI *Dune* holds up very well as spectacle because of its superlative design and unusual effects; the scenes of the Guild Navigators, the folding of time, the roaring giant worms emerging from the sand and the vast scaffolds in space all retain the sense of enormous scale and wonder, requiring months of painstaking work. Similarly the matte paintings – by Master of the Matte Albert Whitlock – are nothing short of superb, although the film certainly is let down by some truly dreadful blue-screen compositing.

Matters are hardly helped by the score. Science fiction scores generally range from the orchestral (*2001 A Space Odyssey* [1968], *Star Wars*) to the otherworldly (*Forbidden Planet* [1956]). One would have thought that Lynch would be pleased to populate his film with the mood noises and soundscapes he often employs. While the main theme by the variable genius Brian Eno is perfectly acceptable, all credibility vanishes whenever Toto's painfully pompous bombastic prog-rock drivel crashes in. It manages simultaneously to cheapen and date the film, with quite breathtaking ease.

Ultimately *Dune* remains an oddity in the Lynch canon. Wildly ambitious, visually sumptuous and with a dense narrative, it falters at times under its own audacity. It's easy to blame the producers, who had more input than Lynch had previously been used to, but there really was little that could be done to improve the film. Various 'lost' and 'extended' prints have been mentioned through the years and a number of extended television cuts have been released. These were produced long after the original film, containing outtakes and even storyboards of scenes that were never shot. Lynch has had his name removed from all subsequent versions.

YOU STAY ALIVE, BABY. DO IT FOR VAN GOGH.

Critically *Dune* was met with bemusement and some vitriol. Commercially the film failed to recoup its shooting budget and placed the Dino de Laurentiis Corporation in financial trouble. Yet the company stuck by their director and bankrolled a modestly budgeted production on which they would grant Lynch complete creative control. That film was *Blue Velvet*.

Blue Velvet (1986)

Directed by: David Lynch
Written by: David Lynch
Produced by: Fred C Caruso
Edited by: Duwayne Dunham
Cinematography: Frederick Elmes
Music by: Angelo Badalamenti
Cast: Isabella Rossellini (Dorothy Vallens), Kyle MacLachlan (Jeffrey Beaumont), Dennis Hopper (Frank Booth), Laura Dern (Sandy Williams), Hope Lange (Mrs Williams), Dean Stockwell (Ben), George Dickerson (Detective Williams), Priscilla Pointer (Mrs Beaumont), Frances Bay (Aunt Barbara), Jack Harvey (Tom Beaumont), Brad Dourif (Raymond), Jack Nance (Paul), Fred Pickler (Yellow Man), Angelo Badalamenti (Piano Player)

Welcome to the bright and cheery town of Lumberton, where they have more wood than a woodchuck chucks. Jeffrey Beaumont returns from college to look after the family hardware store when his father suffers a stroke. On his way home from the hospital, Jeffrey finds a human ear and takes it to Detective Williams. Williams' daughter, Sandy, tells him about her father's cases and that one involves a nightclub singer, Dorothy Vallens, who lives nearby. Intrigued, Jeffrey breaks into Dorothy's apartment to find out more, but is discovered by her. Another visitor arrives and Jeffrey's bundled into a closet, where he watches the loathsome Frank Booth abuse Dorothy. It appears that Frank has kidnapped her husband and child and is using them as bargaining chips to allow him violent sexual access to her.

Jeffrey tells Sandy, and she is both fascinated and repelled. They both visit the nightclub to see Dorothy sing. Later, Sandy tells Jeffrey of a dream she had about robins bringing happiness to the world. Jeffrey continues his investigation and follows Frank from the nightclub, taking photos of his dealings with a man in a yellow jacket. Jeffrey returns to Dorothy's apartment later that evening and they make love, she begging him to hit her. As he leaves, Frank shows up and takes them both for a joyride. Frank becomes increasingly confrontational, taunting Jeffrey and Dorothy. Eventually, Jeffrey can take no more and hits Frank, who then turns on him savagely. The next day, Jeffrey tells Sandy about the incident and they agree that things have gone too far. He visits the police station, but spots the Yellow Man in one of the offices.

After a party, Sandy and Jeffrey declare their love for each other but arrive home to find Dorothy on Jeffrey's front lawn, naked and delirious. They call for an ambulance and Dorothy makes it known that Jeffrey has slept with her. Although Sandy is appalled and distraught, she forgives him. Jeffrey takes Dorothy to the hospital then goes to her apartment, ensuring that Detective Williams knows of his whereabouts. There he finds the earless Don Vallens and the Yellow Man, both dead. Jeffrey learns from the police radio that Frank is on his way to the apartment but tricks him and hides in the closet. As Frank opens the door, Jeffrey blows his brains out. Back home, Sandy spots a robin in the garden.

Blue Velvet is Lynch's first film to scratch explicitly beneath the surface of normality. Innocent youths confront the expansive, mysterious and dangerous world that exists outside their homogenised lives and characters slowly begin to realise that the world isn't full of apple pie and nice robins. The chance discovery of an ear leads Jeffrey to realise his potential as an investigator, aided and abetted by Sandy. Central to the mystery is Dorothy, eking out a meagre existence in an apartment, abused by kidnapping psychopath Frank Booth. But Jeffrey's probing into Dorothy's life is more than altruistic; he makes the fundamental error of becoming emotionally involved in his case with tragic consequences. His redemption, and that of Dorothy, can only come from his innocence and the knowledge that true love can prevail.

At a pivotal point in his life, Jeffrey is discovering both the confusion and responsibility that surrounds late puberty. He is no longer a child and must enter the world of adulthood. This is partly brought about by necessity. His father has suffered a terrible stroke, forcing him to leave college. Suddenly he is the man of the family and the hardware store has become his responsibility, even if it is, for all intents and purposes, run by his father's employees. When he returns home after being savagely beaten by Frank, as the head of the house (rather than stroppy teenager) he insists that his mother and aunt do not talk about it. The beating marks his final initiation into manhood. The culmination of the end of his youth is also demonstrated through his awakening sexual urges, denied by the chaste but wanting Sandy and satiated by the lonely, vulnerable and masochistic Dorothy. Dorothy offers an adult sexuality far beyond Jeffrey's knowledge and awakens desires and demons he does not realise he has in him. His outward goodness, his desire for the pure love that Sandy seems to offer him (let's not forget that Sandy, the robin-loving, doe-eyed, so-called innocent is cheating on her boyfriend and is ultimately the catalyst for the turmoil that engulfs Jeffrey's life) masks an inner self that can spiral into the kind of sadism that Frank represents. While Jeffrey can never be the sadistic Frank, his beating of Dorothy shows us that he is capable of such acts. Is he any better than Frank? The difference is that Jeffrey shows remorse for his actions; he is not an id run amuck, uncontrolled and volatile. He has the potential, as do we all, to carry out unspeakable things but he curtails it and repents of his sins. Ultimately this erosion of his middle-class inhibitions, the realisation that he is capable of acts he thought impossible, gives him the strength to unleash the fatal shot into Frank's forehead.

A key theme is that of voyeurism and how the watcher can become tainted by the subject. *Blue Velvet* extends this to the viewer as the love of watching – the illicit and sexual thrill – provides joy and danger to the character and, ultimately, the audience. There is a sense in which the audience is playing the role of passive voyeur, safe in the knowledge that events on the screen don't affect them, that they are undetectable. Lynch's characters have a similar feeling of invulnerability, as though their inquisitive natures and youthful innocence provide a protective coat that shields them from discovery. Of course this proves not to be the case for either the protagonists or the audience, who also contribute emotional baggage and responses to the onscreen events, albeit to a far lesser extent. But then this is what cinema is about – emotional response. Jeffrey has an excuse for his indiscretions. He could argue that he had no intention of spying on Dorothy but the fact remains that he breaks into her apartment and watches, as we do, the abuse Frank perpetrates. He could look away. He could intervene (which the audience, short of walking out, cannot). But instead he is compelled to watch a sexual assault, impotent but transfixed. It is the realisation that the wholesome can be corrupted by exposure to the darkness.

But Jeffrey goes further, taking advantage of Dorothy's weakness, her need to be loved, and using it for his own sexual needs. He has been contaminated by exposure. As Frank rather exaggerates, 'You are like me'. Later Dorothy will declare to a distraught Sandy that 'he put his disease in me' but the term is more than a euphemism for his sperm. Jeffrey has become tainted, infected by the seedier side of life that was bubbling away close to home and within his own psyche. This duality of good and corrupted innocence crops up in many of Lynch's characters, notably Laura Palmer.

In many respects Jeffrey is a more simplistic character than Sandy, living out his *Boys' Own* dreams and discovering a dark sexuality of which he was either unaware or in denial. Sandy is less reactive than Jeffrey, living her fantasies by proxy. As such she coerces Jeffrey to do what she wants by appealing to his sense of discovery and mystery. As the daughter of a policeman she has acquired her father's need to solve crimes but also inherited his hands-off approach to detection, letting the underlings do the footwork. While she is appalled at the naked Dorothy vouching for Jeffrey's semen, her shock isn't only at Jeffrey's infidelity (arguably they weren't going out when Jeffrey first had sex with Dorothy) but at the fact that, deep down, she is aware that she was complicit in the relationship. It is Sandy who tells Jeffrey about Dorothy's connection to the severed ear case, Sandy who tells him where Dorothy lives and who helps him break into the apartment. All through the film she subtly steers Jeffrey in the direction of a solution while, for the most part, shying away from confronting the truth directly. For that to happen, the mystery – Dorothy – must come to her.

Blue Velvet continues Lynch's very particular use of diegetic sound and songs, putting both centre stage, integral to the characters as well as the audience. This is partly due to the film's foregrounding of the theatrical, but also in the characters' relationships with, and reaction to, songs. In *Blue Velvet* this is most prevalent because one of the lead players is a singer. In *Twin Peaks* Julee Cruise's songs emotionally affect and reflect the lives of the townspeople, but Dorothy is far more integrated into the text. It is her song that gives the film its title and Frank one of his numerous sexual quirks. It also unites the four main protagonists spatially, at the nightclub, for the only time in the film. Frank's association with songs seems to motivate his actions – *Blue Velvet* represents his sexual urges – but there is also the use of Roy Orbison's *In Dreams*, an apt title for a song in a David Lynch film. Initially performed as a mime by Frank's friend Ben, Frank makes it his own when spitting out the lyrics to the captured Jeffrey. It is here that he also vents the lines, 'Don't be a good neighbour to her or I'm gonna send you a love letter. Straight from my heart, fucker. You know what a love letter is? It's a bullet. Straight from my gun, fucker'. These statements are underlined when the track *Love Letters Straight from Your Heart* plays over the hail of bullets during the police raid. In some ways, Frank's words have reflected reality.

The use of lyrics to attach characters to the film soundtrack continues through most of Lynch's work, from Sailor's rendition of *Love Me Tender* to the Mystery Man's recollection of *Song to the Siren* – a song initially intended for *Blue Velvet* but deemed too expensive at the time. *Blue Velvet* also marks Lynch's first collaboration with Angelo Badalamenti, who was initially called in to help Isabella Rossellini sing the titular song, but also ended up writing the music to Lynch's lyrics for *The Mysteries of Love*. Badalamenti has scored most of Lynch's subsequent films.

In dreams Lynch can be his most lyrical and infuriating. Despite the film's dreamlike appearance, *Blue Velvet* is unusual in that dreams do not overtly manifest themselves; the closest we get are Sandy's recollections of the robins. Instead Lynch falls upon another way to alter our perception of events – memory. In principle, memory shouldn't be fundamentally different from related cinematic techniques such as flashbacks but in the Lynch film it acts as a form of wakened dreaming about past events. Normally dreams are clues to mysteries or portents of the future, and this is especially true in *Dune* and *Twin Peaks,* which both feature dreaming as intrinsic to their meaning. We understand that dreams can be illogical, emotional or elliptical, but so too can memory. Memories have an in-built subjectivity depending on the person remembering. But this doesn't always make things better. Following a tempestuous night sleeping with Dorothy, Jeffrey finds unwanted memories flooding back to his mind as he recalls repeatedly hitting her. These are distorted re-runs of events that we have 'witnessed' earlier, here contaminated by Jeffrey's regret and self-loathing at such actions. A similar event, though more pleasant to the person remembering, occurs in *Lost Highway* when

Pete remembers seeing Alice to the strains of Lou Reed's *This Magic Moment*. He has taken one isolated glimpse at a pretty girl and woven it into an extended, improperly remembered fantasy.

The fictional Lumberton is a sleepy logging town that hides dark secrets. This delineation is profound not only in the contrasts between good and evil or day and night but also in the architecture that separates the two societies that co-exist in the town: the middle class picket-fenced citizens of the day and the industrial apartment dwellers of the night. The film's opening shots show us only the daytime, the world of cheery neighbours and apple pie, where the firemen wave and the gardens are meticulously tended; an American idyll that is just a block from the American nightmare, seemingly unaware of its co-existence. The stroke suffered by Jeffrey's father provides the catalyst for these worlds to collide, for it is on the journey to and from the hospital that Jeffrey is forced to step outside his own homogenised piece of America. The severed ear in the field by the forest leads him into the murky world of Frank Booth.

Frank Booth is one of cinema's most memorable villains – a pantomime hoodlum warped by perversity into a figure of utter, irredeemable immorality. He is an id let free in a world of darkness that embraces the evil and abuses the good. He sees no problem in kidnapping a small child and chopping off his father's ear in order to have abusive sex with Dorothy. He's so tied up in his own behavioural desires that he becomes infant-like in his needs and demands, even reverting to crude approximations of a childhood either denied or remembered in order to allow him free expression of his deviant needs. 'Mommy. Baby wants to fuck.' He is clearly relating to an Oedipal need to fuck his mother and usurp his father, even to become his father – 'Daddy's home!' To fund his lifestyle Frank is a criminal and as such he surrounds himself with criminal elements. These are every bit as odd as Frank himself: the misfits Paul and Raymond and the brothel owner cum drug dealer Ben, a pasty-faced 'suave fucker' with a penchant for mime and sudden violence. It is well-documented that Dennis Hopper telephoned Lynch declaring himself to be Frank Booth, but another actor, Robert

Loggia, was after the role. While Hopper got the part and made the role his own, Loggia's anger at missing out eventually fed into his performance as another of Lynch's finest villains – Mr Eddy from *Lost Highway*. *Blue Velvet* is considered by many to be Lynch's finest hour, the film where he perfectly merged the normal with the abnormal, brought surrealism into the sunshine and produced a deeply disturbing film that demands multiple viewings. On first viewing it appears to be a simple, if warped, detective story. But, like Jeffrey Beaumont's investigations, it's a multi-layered affair and, despite moments of mirth, remains a highly disquieting experience. Critical responses to the film were mixed on its release, but it garnered an Oscar® nomination for Lynch. Its status as one of the true masterpieces of modern cinema was confirmed in 2002 when magazine *Sight & Sound* placed it fifth in its top ten films of the previous 25 years.

Following the success of *Blue Velvet*, Lynch was invited to Paris to discuss the possibility of filming a short piece over dinner with Daniel Toscan du Plantier. France's *Figaro* magazine was commissioning directors to make short films in commemoration of their tenth anniversary. All the shorts would be on the open theme of 'France as seen by…' ('Les Français vus par') with Lynch representing America. Other collaborators would include Werner Herzog, Andrzej Wajda and, in a post-modern twist, Jean-Luc Godard. Initially Lynch declined but had a change of heart and agreed to do the film, pitching the idea of *The Cowboy and the Frenchman*. Daniel Toscan du Plantier agreed, enthusing 'two clichés in one'.[13]

The Cowboy and the Frenchman (1988)

Directed by: David Lynch
Written by: David Lynch
Cast: Harry Dean Stanton (Slim), Frederic Golchan (Pierre the Frenchman), Jack Nance (Pete), Tracey Walter (Dusty), Rick Guillory (Howdy), Michael Horse (Broken Feather)

'What the hell is that damn thing?' asks hardened cowboy Slim of the shape that is struggling through the grassy hills of his ranch. He sends Pete and Dusty to lasso what turns out to be a wide-eyed Frenchman wandering the plains. Inside his voluminous valise are a number of items including wine, baguettes, Camembert, escargots and French fries. The cowboys realise he is French and not an 'alien spy', and welcome him, unaware that they are being stalked by an American Indian. It turns out that the Indian has been trailing the Frenchman for ten days out of curiosity. As night falls, the group are served beer and food by cowgirls and enjoy a variety show of increasingly bizarre acts as drunkenness sets in. A chorus of *Home on the Range* and a rousing cheer of 'Vive la France' leads to a morning after of new cultural understanding…

The film marks a return to the silent style of comedy that often becomes sinister in Lynch's work. He even starts the film with a title card and ends with an iris-out shot, further creating an impression of a link to cinema's bygone age. Here the effect is pure slapstick, in a manner that would become apparent in the unsuccessful television series *On the Air*. The character of Slim with his poor hearing provides the basis, for the similarly afflicted Gordon Cole in *Twin Peaks*. Harry Dean Stanton's deadpan, 1950s-style cussing cowboy repeats phrases *ad nauseam* and seems generally bemused at every foreign artefact dragged from the beleaguered Frenchman's deceptively large suitcase. Essentially this is a simple comedy of culture clashes. Slim's existence is so contained he has no understanding of anything that doesn't fit his tunnel view of the world. His companions Pete and Dusty are similarly bemused, especially at the snails – 'maybe he fell asleep by a stream' – so that we are to 'see the French' in terms of what makes them different from this idealised notion of the free American cowboy. Lynch uses the trappings of the cowboy film to create a piece of 'nostalgia', complete with a singing chorus of girls marking the passing of time and sepia-tinged cinematography. In this context he can justify the archaic and basic use of comedy as symptomatic of an idealised past. The Frenchman himself is a more traditionally comic character – pasty-faced with a habit of shuffling his feet when agitated – an amalgam of Charlie Chaplin and Jacques Tati by way of the Surrealists.

While *The Cowboy and the Frenchman* starts as a simple, if bizarre, farce, it soon descends into a cavalcade of the absurd. Rearing horses, can-can dancers by firelight, an Elvis-style country rock star and all manner of entertainments blur in a Fellini-esque parade of juxtaposed sound and vision.

This was to mark the first time Lynch had worked on video since the *Amputee* experiment but he still retained the services of long-time collaborator Frederick Elmes and assistant Catherine Coulson. It was around this time that the 'Lynch Mob', as it became known, would really start coming together, a group of collaborators that would work with Lynch on multiple projects. Patricia Norris, production designer on *Blue Velvet* and soon to be a regular fixture in his future work was also present, as was the ever-popular Jack Nance. New to the stable were cult favourite Harry Dean Stanton as the bellowing Slim and Michael Horse (Broken Feather), who would later prove to be a valuable ally for the forces of good in *Twin Peaks*, as tracker extraordinaire Deputy Hawk.

The Cowboy and the Frenchman provides the genesis for many later works, often in the details. The absurdist humour would go some way to give *Twin Peaks* its edge amidst the dark revelations and soap opera trappings. The gastronomic psychotic Jerry Horne's obsession with cheese finds its roots here, a fixation that also permeates the unfilmed Frost collaboration *One Saliva Bubble*. The use of cowboys in a modern context is given a more sinister edge in *Mulholland Dr.*

Ultimately *The Cowboy and the Frenchman* represents little more than a curio but its importance lies in the genesis of different directions in Lynch's work, the emergence of a team of collaborators and as a foray into the world of television.

THE WAY YOUR HEAD WORKS IS GOD'S OWN PRIVATE MYSTERY

The years surrounding 1990 saw Lynch at his most prolific and productive. He had met Mark Frost and formed a working relationship culminating in the filming of the *Twin Peaks* pilot. *Twin Peaks,* the series, was about to hit the world's television screens big time, but Lynch was still actively pursuing cinema projects and found a window of opportunity to make *Wild at Heart.*

Wild at Heart (1990)

Directed by: David Lynch
Written by: David Lynch from the novel by Barry Gifford
Produced by: Steve Golin, Monty Montgomery, Sigurjon Sighvatsson
Edited by: Duwayne Dunham
Cinematography: Frederick Elmes
Music: Angelo Badalamenti
Cast: Nicolas Cage (Sailor Ripley), Laura Dern (Lula Pace Fortune), Willem Dafoe (Bobby Peru), Diane Ladd (Marietta Pace Fortune), JE Freeman (Santos), Isabella Rossellini (Perdita Durango), Harry Dean Stanton (Johnnie Farragut), Grace Zabriskie (Juana), Sherilyn Fenn (Girl in Accident), Crispin Glover (Cousin Dell), Calvin Lockhart (Reggie), Marvin Kaplan (Uncle Pooch), William Morgan Sheppard (Mr Reindeer), Freddie Jones (George Kovich), Jack Nance (00 Spool), Sheryl Lee (Glinda, the Good Witch)

At a party in Cape Fear, Sailor is accused of assaulting Lula's mother by Bob Ray Lemon, who draws a knife. Sailor defends himself, brutally beating and smashing his assailant's head into the marble floor. Months later, despite desperate pleas from her mother that she should never see Sailor again, Lula is reunited with her man as he is released from the Pee Dee Correctional Institution. Sailor and Lula make passionate love, then go dancing. Lula's mother, Marietta, is beside herself with rage and entreats part-time lover Johnnie Farragut to find Lula and bring her home. She also enlists the assistance of her dubious associate Santos to kill Sailor. Santos' price is that he gets to kill Farragut too, although he ensures that the killings are arranged by Mr Reindeer, so as not to appear directly involved. Marietta has a crisis of conscience and warns Johnnie, but she is too late and he is killed in a bizarre voodoo ritual.

Sailor breaks parole and heads for California with his girl. Running short of money they reach the town of Big Tuna and meet the repugnant Bobby Peru. Lula reveals to Sailor that she is pregnant. Bobby figures this out and persuades Sailor to help in an armed robbery in order to finance his family. But the heist is a set-up and Peru is working for Santos. Peru shoots the clerks then turns on Sailor, whose gun is full of dummy bullets. However, the police show up and in the ensuing chaos Peru blows his own head clean away. Sailor gives himself up and is sent to jail.

Years later Pace, Sailor's son, and Lula travel to meet him. Their encounter is awkward and Sailor decides it would be best if he leaves them. But Glinda, the Good Witch, tells him that Lula loves him and the family reunite.

The first of the six short novels by Barry Gifford, *Wild at Heart* tells the story of Sailor and Lula and their adventures on the run through a sprawling American landscape. Like much of Gifford's work it is rich with incidental detail and perfectly formed mini-biographies. Gifford's world is one in which everything is connected, however obtusely, and all the characters, to some extent, have equal weight. Despite the brevity of the books such a vast cast of identifiable characters could prove problematic for a big screen adaptation but Gifford's characters are all so plausibly quirky that differentiation is not a problem. What is remarkable about David Lynch's adaptation is how closely the film sticks to the events of the novel, embellishing some sections (notably the killing of Bob Ray Lemon) and adding a few of the director's own quirks (the old men in the New Orleans hotel lobby and Freddie Jones talking backwards for no readily apparent reason). Most importantly, much of the dialogue from the novel runs intact and Lynch uses these interchanges to expand the film's world. Often a character will begin an anecdote which allows Lynch the opportunity to cut away to what is effectively a narrated vignette, a mini side story that tries to make sense of a chaotic but connected world.

Unlike the characters that populate Lynch's other films there is no separation of class and no dark secrets that lie beneath the surface. Yes there are mysteries, in that the characters' pasts are revealed during the course of the film, but these are more open, because in Sailor and Lula's world there are no illusions of stability. Everyone is searching for a better life but it is just that, a better one, not a mythologised idea of the American middle-class idyll. In *Blue Velvet* and *Twin Peaks* the shell of respectability is shown to be just that, a fragile boundary that marks the rottenness inside, but in *Wild at Heart* there is no shell to penetrate. Both Sailor and Lula are aware of the cruelties and unfairness of the world – they just have to accept it and move on. Lula is almost matter-of-fact about her rape at the hands of the loathsome Uncle Pooch when she was a child. She has on the surface reduced the rape to just another incident in her life.

What contradicts this is that Lynch shows the deep pain behind her apparently emotionless monologue by showing her actual recollection of events. Rather than depict this as a conventional flashback with voiceover, instead we see the young Lula as a baby doll version of her current adult self. Rather than use a child actor in the role Lynch shows how relevant the incident is to Lula while also noting how memory is altered by time, providing an unreliable witness to events. A similar discrepancy occurs when Lula discusses her abortion, provided by her mother with dispassionate professionalism, in that her description is at odds with her recollection of it. What makes the film work so tightly is the way in which these apparently isolated vignettes eventually tie together to give the bigger picture. These fragments have led Sailor and Lula to the place they now inhabit, a life on the run. But the key to *Wild at Heart* is their relationship, which is intense and passionate. They are young, sexy and, above all, very deeply in love.

If there is a main theme to *Wild at Heart* it is that of fire. The opening credits emphasise the aesthetics of pyrotechnic destruction: the shots of burning, extreme close-ups of a lighting match, the crackle of an inhaled cigarette, the tumbling shots of amber consummation. Fire, as in *Fire Walk With Me*, can serve evil as well as good. It defines a number of key elements within the film: Lula's father dies brutally in a fire, and Sherilyn Fenn's car crash victim stumbles around incoherently while the shattered remains of her last ride burns in the background. But fire isn't only seen as bad, it fuels Sailor and Lula's passion, right down to their frequent post-coital cigarettes that smoulder and glow across the screen.

Perhaps the more audacious elements of the film are the overt references to *The Wizard of Oz* (1939). Whilst this is not unique (John Waters similarly used much of the film in his cult classic *Female Trouble* [1974]) it is unusual that they are so blatant, so transparent to the audience. Indeed the whole fantasy element was one of the many things that divided audiences and critics upon the film's initial release. Referencing other works in a film usually ranges from the recycling of scenes to outright homage. There's also the sly nod, a knowing reference that will either be understood or ignored. Ultimately this is an 'in joke', a piece of movie trivia given a sense of post-modern respectability through its association with previous iconography. *Wild at Heart* adopts *The Wizard of Oz* almost as its template of existence, a warped and mutated offspring that appears on the surface to be as far removed from its progenitor as could be imagined, yet ultimately has the same yearning for normality. Like Dorothy in *Blue Velvet*, Sailor and Lula come to realise that what they want is stability, away from the fantastical madness around them, the knowledge that love conquers all and a sense that a wholesome, anonymous life of mediocrity is a laudable goal. In this respect, both films can be seen as intrinsically reactionary in that they tell the audience to accept their place in society.

With that in mind the *Wizard of Oz* links become all the more relevant: Marietta is an incestuous mirror of the Wicked Witch of the West, cackling wildly, pursuing the couple on her broom, gazing into her crystal ball or sending her 'lovelies' off to do her bidding. The fact that she remains for the most part housebound shows how much her survival has relied on others while she manipulates events from afar. Glinda, the Good Witch, remains almost identical to her Oz counterpart but similarly instigates a mostly hands-off approach. The symbiosis between the films doesn't just occur on a character level but with the dialogue too, with key lines appropriated or manipulated to represent Sailor and Lula's yearnings and emotions in their inverted fairytale world, offering hope or providing wry commentary. 'It sure as hell ain't the Emerald City,' Sailor notes of Big Tuna. Yet the whole point, in this instance, is that he is wrong. Big Tuna is as artificial, with just as many things going on behind closed doors. Like the Emerald City it offers none of the protection the characters hope for. Bobby Peru tempts Sailor into robbery by suggesting that monetary gain would help him and his pregnant girlfriend 'down that yellow brick road', which proves prophetic for ultimately the yellow brick road doesn't lead to a solution, it is just a direction. Similarly Lula taps her red shoes together three times in the hope that she can be whisked away from her present plight and find her heart's desire, but to no avail.

Lynch populates his films with characters who control the lives of others, whilst remaining separate from them. In *Wild at Heart* Mr Reindeer is a Buñuelian crime lord with sinister motives and a predilection for surrounding himself in scantily clad servants. His status as someone who is seemingly above retribution is repeated in the figures of Mr Eddy in *Lost Highway* and *Mulholland Dr.*'s Mr Roque. *Twin*

Peaks' Ben Horne's aspirations of such dominance are amateur at best, his sexual appetites whetted by (initially) willing prostitutes at One Eyed Jack's a far cry from the dark sexuality, dominance and subjugation exercised by his counterparts.

Wild at Heart is the first of what we might call Lynch's road movie trilogy, the other two being *Lost Highway* and *The Straight Story*, a triptych of films that explore different elements of that loosely connected sub-genre. *Wild at Heart* follows a tradition of 'couples on the run' films typified by such movies as Hitchcock's *Young and Innocent* (1937) or *The 39 Steps* (1935). It differs in that the authority figure from whom the couple flee is closer to home. *Wild at Heart* also shows an affinity to the crime-spree couple films typified by Arthur Penn's *Bonnie and Clyde* (1967) and Terrence Malick's *Badlands* (1974) – particularly the latter's use of character narration, which complements but does not match the action. In turn, the influence of *Wild at Heart* on later examples of the genre is pronounced, most notably on Quentin Tarantino's oeuvre and Oliver Stone's hyperactive *Natural Born Killers* (1994) with its similarly eclectic use of music (although some would argue Stone's film is far less coherent on every level). As a road movie, incidental events punctuate the proceedings – in one scene reminiscent of Godard's 'road movie as anti-capitalist diatribe' *Weekend* (1967) the couple come across the scene of a terrible car crash. The only survivor may well be alive, but she will not live long, for her head injuries are too terrible. At once we know that the road not only offers openness and freedom, an escape for our lovers, but also the threat of death. At the film's close (and in another nod to *Weekend*) a traffic jam, the very antithesis of the road movie, allows the couple to reunite. Their journey to the heart of darkness has ended; their new life has just begun.

Despite a mixed critical reaction at the time *Wild at Heart* received the coveted *Palme d'Or* at the Cannes Film Festival.

THIS MUST BE WHERE PIES GO WHEN THEY DIE

In some sense *Twin Peaks* marks Lynch at his most successful for, despite the critical appreciation of his films, *Twin Peaks* infiltrated an audience who were unaware of his other work and unlikely to seek it out. Audiences worldwide had the strange and wonderful world of David Lynch beamed directly into their homes and, for a while at least, it gripped the imagination of people who would never dream of seeing *Blue Velvet* or *Eraserhead*.

Twin Peaks (1990)

Directed by: Graeme Clifford, Caleb Deschanel, Duwayne Dunham, Ulrich Edel, James Foley, Mark Frost, Lesli Linka Glatter, Stephen Gyllenhaal, Todd Holland, Tim Hunter, Diane Keaton, David Lynch, Tina Rathborne, Jonathan Sanger

Cast: Kyle MacLachlan (Dale Cooper), Michael Ontkean (Sheriff Harry S Truman), Mädchen Amick (Shelly Johnson), Dana Ashbrook (Bobby Briggs), Richard Beymer (Benjamin Horne), Lara Flynn Boyle (Donna Hayward), Sherilyn Fenn (Audrey Horne), Warren Frost (Dr Hayward), Peggy Lipton (Norma Jennings), James Marshall (James Hurley), Everett McGill (Big Ed Hurley), Jack Nance (Pete Martell), Ray Wise (Leland Palmer), Piper Laurie (Catherine Martell), Michael J Anderson (The Man from Another Place), Phoebe Augustine (Ronette Pulaski), Ian Buchanan (Richard Tremayne), Joan Chen (Josie Packard), Catherine E Coulson (The Log Lady), Eric DaRe (Leo Johnson), Don Davis (Major Briggs), Miguel

Ferrer (Albert Rosenfield), Harry Goaz (Andy Brennan), Heather Graham (Annie Blackburn), Michael Horse (Deputy 'Hawk'), David Patrick Kelly (Jerry Horne), Sheryl Lee (Laura Palmer/Madeleine Ferguson), David Lynch (Gordon Cole), Chris Mulkey (Hank Jennings), Walter Olkewicz (Jacques Renault), Kimmy Robertson (Lucy Moran), Wendy Robie (Nadine Hurley), Russ Tamblyn (Doctor Jacoby), Frank Silva (Bob), Lenny von Dohlen (Harold Smith), Al Strobel (Mike/The One Armed Man), Kenneth Welsh (Windom Earle), Grace Zabriskie (Sarah Palmer)

The body of local schoolgirl Laura Palmer is found washed up on a lake-side shore, wrapped in plastic. Laura, who bears an uncanny resemblance to her cousin Maddy, is the daughter of lawyer Leland and Sarah Palmer, and the best friend of Donna Hayward, daughter of Doctor and Eileen Hayward and sister of goody-goodies Gersten and Harriet, who is dating Mike, friend of Laura's boyfriend Bobby Briggs, son of Major and Mrs Briggs, who is secretly seeing waitress Shelly Johnson, who works alongside giggling Heidi at the Double R Diner owned by Norma Jennings, whose husband Hank is on parole for manslaughter, a crime that could become murder if he succeeds in his hit on Shelly's husband Leo Johnson, loathsome buddy of fat barman Jacques Renault, whose equally dubious brothers Bernard and Jean have nefarious connections with Blackie, the madam at the local brothel One Eyed Jack's, owned by local entrepreneur and hotelier Benjamin Horne, brother of hyperactive globetrotter gourmet Jerry, father of sultry and sneaky Audrey and psychiatrist hippy Dr Lawrence Jacoby's patient Johnny, and husband of Sylvia despite his extra-marital bedhopping and plotting with Catherine Martell, wife of long-suffering Pete Martell and sister of the late Andrew Packard, whose widow Josie owns the local saw mill and is now dating Sheriff Harry S Truman, head of the local police station and boss to lovers Deputy Andy Brennan and Lucy Moran, and secret society protector along with Deputy Hawk and gas station owner Ed Hurley who, with drape-obsessed mono-sighted wife Nadine, is guardian to brooding biker James Hurley, who was secretly having a relationship with Laura Palmer, whose death is being investigated by FBI Agent Dale Cooper, ably assisted by no-nonsense colleague Albert Rosenfield and painfully-short-of-hearing boss, Gordon Cole in an esoteric way involving dreams of giants, owls and a killer, Bob, whose partner Mike may hold the clue to the murder... And then there's the Log Lady.[14]

The quiet town of Twin Peaks, population 51,200 give or take, would seem an unlikely setting for murder, drugs and passionate affairs but underpinning its sleepy exterior are the evil doings in the forest that seep into its corners and affect the lives of everyone, even outsiders, who come into its luscious folds. Quiet town? Twin Peaks may be a place where an orange light means slow down not speed up but there's far more to it than meets the eye. Leland's hair turns white. Nadine's super-human powers and belief that she's 18 have resulted from an overdose of sleeping pills due to the failure of her invention of silent drape runners. There's a killer chess game. What's with the one-armed shoe-seller and his addiction to bizarre drug cocktails? Ben Horne's business dealings, both legitimate and otherwise, result in a sharp character change from brothel owner and plotter to post-Civil War carrot-munching defender of the endangered pine weasel. Whatever happened to Ronette Pulaski? Will the Mayor stay with the woman who killed his brother through over-stimulating sex? Why does Josie become part of the furniture? What's in Owl Cave? What is the Black Lodge and where is it? How long can Leo grit his teeth? A kid'll eat ivy too, wouldn't you?

At its height *Twin Peaks* fever reached a hysterical pitch in the US, UK and Japan, and the phrase 'Who killed Laura Palmer?' was on everyone's lips. In the US the pilot was watched by a third of all viewers and UK audience figures for the show (which was broadcast on BBC2 and not on the mainstream BBC1) sometimes topped seven million, a figure that few series on any channel can reach these days. Like much of Lynch's output this is about dark secrets that exist in apparently wholesome places. Although working in the confines of mainstream television resulted in some sacrifices – the terrestrial networks in the US

(*Twin Peaks* was broadcast by ABC) have very strict guidelines on bad language, sex and nudity – in many ways these restrictions are what give the series its edge. Sadly the enthusiasm for the series was short lived. Audience share took a sharp downward turn halfway through Season Two but, while it lasted, *Twin Peaks* was the *de rigueur* show to watch, and be seen watching, its coffee culture spurring many a workplace discussion.

In many respects television is more of a group effort than film – with its tighter shooting schedules and fast writing turnaround, it's a more collaborative medium. The genesis of *Twin Peaks* and its distinctive style owes much to the Lynch factor but it is important to recognise everyone's input on the show – notably co-creator Mark Frost and writers Harley Peyton and Robert Engels (who also co-authored *Fire Walk With Me*). Lynch and Frost had collaborated before, developing a number of screenplays together, and their ability to work closely gave *Twin Peaks* the perfect springboard. Frost had worked extensively on television, writing scripts for shows such as *Hill Street Blues*, and was familiar with the formats of TV drama – formats he was particularly eager to break away from.

Lynch had never worked in television but was intrigued by the possibilities the medium offered – the chance to explore the minutia of life, allowing stories to evolve over a more languid timeframe than a feature film; and this is apparent in all the episodes of the series that he directed. Yet *Twin Peaks* does have a narrative that is abundant with parallel storylines, requiring plenty of audience attention. Unlike the soap operas that *Twin Peaks* draws much of its character development from (and even pastiches in the *An Invitation to Love* soap that runs in the background of many scenes), this is not a series for dipping into casually. The dense scripting and numerous subplots require mandatory attention to detail. This is both soap opera *in extremis* and *in minutia* – no other soap could get away with the multiple cliff hanger conclusion to series one or spend so much time arguing the merits of pie, donuts and coffee.

Above all else *Twin Peaks* is a programme about mysteries, secrets and emotions. The initial concept of the series, the hook that was used to sell it, was the death of high school homecoming queen Laura Palmer, a basic murder/detective premise. This is probably the greatest television MacGuffin ever. Laura's death is the catalyst for the events that unfold but more important is discovering not how she died or who killed her, but who she was and who the people of Twin Peaks really are. This is a programme about the darkness in the forests and the emotions of the people who live in close proximity. From the outset Lynch shows that this is no ordinary show. Following the discovery of Laura's body 'dead, wrapped in plastic', we witness the grief of an entire town as news of her murder spreads. This is an extraordinarily intimate portrayal of heartache, especially when the lone figure of Sarah Palmer, telephone hanging from the hook, sobs uncontrollably over the death of her daughter. It's a long scene that begins to feel uncomfortable to the viewer; we are used to grief on our television screens being brief or contained, and this raw emotional outpouring is almost unbearable. It is a relief when Special Agent Dale Cooper then appears on the scene. He becomes the audience's guide and we are comforted by his lack of knowledge of the community. Our relationship with Cooper allows us to see into the goodness and sickness of Twin Peaks through objective eyes. Cooper's reliance on the symbolic and incidental gives him a mythical air, which contrasts with his very ordinary appearance – 'FBI standard issue'. His wonderful personality traits lend the series some of its more memorable quotes and humour. His addiction to good coffee – 'black as midnight on a moonless night' – and 'good food, reasonably priced', makes him appear both normal and obsessive.

While Lynch never repeats the sustained mourning of the pilot episode he nevertheless uses television's luxury of time to focus on aspects that are usually rushed in feature films. Nowhere is this more clear than in the opening of *Twin Peaks'* second season when Cooper, having been shot, lies on the floor hoping to get help. At this point the narrative has reached fever pitch – half the major characters are involved in potentially life threatening situations. Normally there would be some resolution or continuation. Instead Lynch slows everything down to match the pace of the geriatric waiter who discovers Cooper, but appears oblivious to his plight. Their painfully slow exchanges create audience tension and frustration, also injecting a large degree of humour.

Lynch directed the pilot and 5 of the 29 episodes that make up the series, all of them pivotal to the overall story. Interestingly, bar the last episode, all occur in the first half of the show. Some have seen this as indicative of the show's decline, suggesting that once the identity of Laura's killer had finally been revealed, the series lost focus and resorted to an over-reliance on comedy sub-plots. It could be argued, however, that this was *Twin Peaks* hitting its stride as the *ne plus ultra* of soap operas, the perfect dissection of conventional soaps' extended plotting cranked into overdrive for absurdist effect. Whatever the result it is undeniable that Lynch's episodes still offer the series' most memorable and startling moments.

Having finished the expensive pilot for the series Lynch was obliged to film a coda to the material for release in the lucrative European market as a standalone film. This version, which went straight to video almost half a year before the pilot was screened in the US, 'explains' the death of Laura Palmer through the roles of Mike and killer Bob, culminating in the Black Lodge sequence where Cooper meets up with Laura and the Man from Another Place. Much of this ending feeds into the later 'official' *Twin Peaks* canon and the film *Fire Walk With Me*. Indeed its inclusion went some way to shaping the myths surrounding Bob, Mike and the Black Lodge that are so ingrained in the series. A highly edited version of this ending forms Cooper's cryptic dream at the end of episode two of the first season (also directed by Lynch); it takes the entire series even to begin unravelling its meaning.

Despite the censorial constraints of terrestrial US television, Lynch pushed the boundaries of what it was acceptable to broadcast on non-subscription channels. Although no sex or nudity is depicted directly in *Twin Peaks* there's an awful lot going on, with infidelity amongst the locals at almost epidemic levels. More importantly the acknowledgement of the shadier side of human sexuality, of sado-masochism, of incestuous rape, prostitution and sexual slavery through heroin addiction plays a part in the series – themes that television executives would usually run a mile from, particularly in relation to a teenage girl. Somehow *Twin Peaks'* combination of quirky surrealism and high production values managed to get such unlikely material past television's moral guardians. Less clear-cut for US stations are depictions of violence. Although overt gore is prohibited, high levels of violence in television shows are largely tolerated. Lynch pushed the boundaries of televisual violence when he came to film the revealing of Laura's killer in episode seven of series two. The next two paragraphs contain spoilers.

One of the most shocking and protracted acts of violence ever committed to television was the killing of Maddy. It is an astonishing and sadistic scene of pure raw emotion – it's as though Lynch listened to the critics who kept moaning about delaying the revelation of Laura's killer and responded by showing it to them brutally and unapologetically. The killer is revealed because he kills again. 'We don't know what will happen or when but there are owls at the Roadhouse.' The Log Lady's statement heralds the awful revelation that follows: at the Roadhouse where Julee Cruise sings, the Giant tells Cooper the news that 'it is happening again'. In previous episodes we had witnessed, confusingly, Sarah Palmer's slow, drugged crawling round her house at night, but not the reason for it. A white horse appears and the record player constantly clicks at the end of its run. It is the soundtrack that will be intercut with Cruise's ethereal singing, elongating the scene to unbearable lengths. Leland stands by the mirror and becomes possessed by evil spirit Bob. Lynch contrasts the staging at the Roadhouse with deliberate use of spotlights to single out Bob on his dreadful mission. Leland is shown to be alternating between himself and Bob by use of jump cuts and editing, a jarring and arresting use of effects. Maddy is brutally beaten, taunted and ravished by the animalistic Bob who growls as he slobbers over her before she is driven head-first into a mirror as the deranged Leland shouts, 'You are going back to Missoula, Montana' – Lynch's birthplace.

Then, in tight close-up mirroring the autopsy scene from the pilot (only in reverse), Leland inserts the letter under Maddy's bloodied fingernail using a scalpel. What is so shocking is not only the brutality of the murder but the length of it – over four minutes of screen time is taken up with this dissection of a killing (most screen murders are seconds in length) and its perverse animal-like carnage. Again mirroring the pilot, Lynch cuts to the Roadhouse. Julee Cruise sings and the waiter/Giant says, 'I'm so sorry'. This causes another emotional outpouring from the townsfolk. Empathetically aware that something tragic has happened, they share a communal grief. It is a remarkable culmination of themes and ideas in its juxtaposition of music, staging, murder and emotion.

The 'revelation of the killer' episode marked a hiatus from the programme for Lynch as director, although he was a regular fixture in front of the camera playing the character of deaf (except around Shelly…) FBI Bureau Chief Gordon Cole. His return to the director's chair ended the series for good and attempted to tie up loose ends in a single show. In many respects this harks back to the European edit and reflects the ultimate fate of *Mulholland Dr.*, with necessity forcing an abrupt conclusion. *Twin Peaks* set the bar for quality television so high it has arguably yet to be bettered or even equalled. It may have eventually alienated its more mainstream audience but, for a short time in 1990, the world was transfixed by the mystery of Laura Palmer and millions of people suddenly found themselves experiencing the bizarre joys of the world of David Lynch.

In addition to his work on *Wild at Heart* and *Twin Peaks*, Lynch also produced an album with Angelo Badalamenti promoting the ethereal tones of singer Julee Cruise. Having worked with the pair on *Blue Velvet*, she became an occasional fixture at *Twin Peaks'* Roadhouse venue and the album *Floating Into the Night* featured tracks from a number of Lynch projects. Most unusual of these was *Industrial Symphony No 1*. Badalamenti had had a long relationship with the Brooklyn Academy of

Music and was approached by them to provide an opening piece for a festival. He discussed this with Lynch and the pair agreed on the title *Industrial Symphony No 1,* preparing the show using a combination of existing Julee Cruise tracks and newly written ones. The result was a multi-media performance piece, using a combination of dance, sculpture, soundscapes and industrial clatter. Having just finished shooting *Wild at Heart* both Laura Dern and Nicolas Cage were available to provide a filmed backstory to the show. The work was performed twice, the video version of which was recorded at the Brooklyn Academy of Music Opera House on November 10 1989 in front of an audience of 2,000. It's easy to see why the idea would be so appealing to Lynch, affording him the opportunity to stage a completely non-narrative installation in a sculpted industrial three-dimensional space unconstrained by the exacting demands of filmmaking. If film can be seen as moving painting *Industrial Symphony No 1* can be viewed as moving sculpture.

Industrial Symphony No 1:
The Dream of the Broken Hearted (1990)

Directed by: David Lynch
Music: David Lynch and Angelo Badalamenti
Cast: Julee Cruise (The Dreamself of the Heartbroken Woman), Laura Dern (Heartbroken Woman), Nicolas Cage (Heartbreaker), Andre Badalamenti (Twin B), Michael J Anderson (Woodbreaker – Twin A)

As a video document of performance art *Industrial Symphony No 1* provides a fascinating glimpse of a world unencumbered by the need for narrative coherence or explanation. Dreams may feature in all Lynch's work but in the context of this musical installation the dream *is* the work. It is not meant to be unravelled or understood in the same way we seek explanation from conventional narrative cinema. Meaning can be sought by the viewer but the overall concern is to create a mood and a feeling, rather than a coherent story. What story there is concerns the dream of a jilted lover, her dreamself represented by Julee Cruise. This gives a hook on which Lynch can attach an industrialised Boschean descent into Hell, self-loathing and despair.

The dream landscape created in *Industrial Symphony No 1* is that of oppressive technology, of the world of industry and manufacture as nightmare. Strobe electricity offers glimpses of the nightmare, crackling and screaming. Oppressive electricity towers and scaffolding surround the stage. The singer is trapped in a car boot and filmed by television cameras, her bleached-out face broadcast to the audience on multiple monitors. Elements of JG Ballard's *Crash* encroach on this world as a half naked girl writhes around the wreck of a car in sexual ecstasy while the falling body of a man tumbles in never-ending torment. Later, in a scene mirrored in *Mulholland Dr.*, a girl masturbates to thoughts of her now departed lover, weeping in shame and frustration while the recollection of their parting is re-enacted by the woodcutter and his twin saxophonist brother. All the while sirens are blaring, recalling *Six Figures Getting Sick*, warning of the impending final battle. This is dark sexual frustration manifesting itself through dreamlike visions.

Recalling the car crash in *Wild at Heart* and predating that of *The Straight Story*, one bizarre incident involves the creation of a giant bipedal skinned deer whose imposing, red seeping frame is kept at bay by hand-held headlights that transfix it. The stark use of red and blue, only disturbed by the white lightning jabs of strobe lighting, lend the piece a dark and oppressive air that is mirrored in many of the dream sequences in Lynch's subsequent works. The difference is that there is no comfortable context within which to relate these images; they just occur, frightening, and without explicit meaning. Juxtaposed with Ms Cruise's dreamy, floating singing and her *Alice in Wonderland* demeanour, the effect is even more unsettling – the soothing, relaxed, somnambulistic light jazz contrasts with the industrial crackles, wails, and screams, shooting flames and the rat-a-tat guns of war planes to disorientate the viewer. As horribly burnt baby dolls hang in the air and the battle commences, the world spins and the nightmarish dream goes on forever.

The sheer scale and ambition of *Industrial Symphony No 1* is remarkable, especially considering the tight schedule for the production. Consolidating many themes from this most productive of periods, elements of the show would resonate in later projects, particularly *Fire Walk With Me* and *Mulholland Dr.*

Despite the sudden demise of the television show, Lynch managed to return to *Twin Peaks* fairly quickly, this time on the big screen with a wider frame and more suitable budget, telling the story of the last few days of Laura Palmer's life. This should have been the first of four films that he would make for CiBy2000 but only *Fire Walk With Me* and *Lost Highway* were filmed. Lynch eventually won substantial damages for breach of contract. Inevitably this commentary of *Fire Walk With Me* contains spoilers.

Twin Peaks: Fire Walk With Me (1992)

Directed by: David Lynch
Written by: David Lynch & Robert Engels
Produced by: Gregg Fienberg, Mark Frost (exec) & David Lynch (exec)
Edited by: Mary Sweeney
Cinematography: Ronald Víctor García
Music: Angelo Badalamenti
Cast: As the television series but with Moira Kelly as Donna Hayward and including David Bowie (Phillip Jeffries), Pamela Gidley (Teresa Banks), Chris Isaak (Chester Desmond), Harry Dean Stanton (Carl Rodd), Kiefer Sutherland (Sam Stanley), Frances Bay (Mrs Tremond/Chalfont)

Teresa Banks is dead, wrapped in plastic, set adrift on a river. FBI boss Gordon Cole assigns Agents Chet Desmond and Sam Stanley to investigate the case. Acting on a hunch they find the letter T on a small piece of paper lodged under the dead girl's fingernail and notice the absence of a ring Teresa had been wearing prior to her murder. Before they can delve further into the mystery Agent Desmond vanishes. Troubled by dreams and ongoing doubts surrounding the case of fellow operative Phillip Jeffries, Special Agent Dale Cooper is given the task of tracing the missing agent's whereabouts. Returning to the trailer park that was Desmond's last known location Cooper finds his car abandoned with the words 'Let's Rock' daubed on the windshield. It becomes clear why this murder is one of Gordon Cole's notorious 'Blue Rose' cases...

One year later, in the quiet town of Twin Peaks, popular schoolgirl Laura Palmer is burning the candle at both ends. She has too many boyfriends, too many classes, too many jobs and a cocaine habit. To add to her burdens she is being molested by a loathsome man named Bob who is even ripping pages from her secret diary – the remainder of which she gives to the reclusive Harold Smith for safekeeping. One day, Laura sees Bob at the foot of her bed. She runs away, and moments later her own father Leland leaves the house.

Donna is trying to understand what is happening to her best friend and follows Laura to a nightclub. It's here that Donna finally begins to see quite how far Laura has spiralled into decadence and self-loathing. Meeting with fellow classmate Ronette Pulaski and the repugnant Jacques Renault she witnesses a world of drink, drugs and casual sex. Narrowly avoiding molestation after her drink has been spiked Donna remembers little of the evening's events.

Out on a drive, Leland and Laura are threatened by Mike, the One Armed Man. Laura confronts Leland about his whereabouts when she spotted Bob in her bedroom and her suspicions become confirmed. That evening, after drugging Laura's mother, Leland rapes her under the guise of Bob.

The next evening, Laura goes with Jacques, Ronette and Leo Johnson to a forest cabin for drugs and sex, unaware that Leland has followed them, waiting for the opportunity to strike. Grabbing the screaming girls, Leland drags them into a nearby railcar and ties them up. The One Armed Man rescues Ronette, but it is too late for Laura, the new owner of Teresa's ring. Murdered by her own possessed father she is wrapped in plastic and set adrift on the river.

Twin Peaks: Fire Walk With Me opens to a screen filled with blue static, a television set without a defined signal and floating random pixel mists of chaos and noise. Similar to the opening credits to *Blue Velvet* this is an undulating river of blue; but rather than offer mystery or sensual feedback, the result here is ominous, aggressive and chaotic. As the camera pulls slowly back the television is violently broken with a baseball bat. *Twin Peaks*, the television series, is shattered on impact. You are not safe in your home, you are in a cinema. This is not going to be an easy, sanitised ride.

From the outset Lynch was determined to place the film as a separate entity from the television series, as a different yet familiar Twin Peaks. It is this very stance – the familiar contrasted with the aggressively altered – that provides the film with both its triumphs and its failures. Audiences need to distance themselves from the television series in order to appreciate the film, but also need familiarity to understand what's happening. Despite the events of the film taking place prior to events in the series knowledge of the entire television show is required. This duality extends throughout *Fire Walk With Me*. Freed of the restrictions of TV, *Fire Walk With Me* depicts all the sex and swearing that the series could only allude to. And Laura herself – the homecoming queen who organises meals on wheels but underneath is a drug addicted, promiscuous girl on the wild side – had to be dead before the pilot even began; her life, as shown in the film, was too wild for television.

Having the (relative) freedom of an R-rating allowed Lynch the opportunity to present a more graphic show for the audience. One good example is in the contrast between the letter-under-the-fingernail scenes. In the series the excruciatingly long sequence, for all its shocking matter-of-factness, mostly makes the viewer squirm because it is protracted and unexpected; for the most part, though, it's conducted in a sanitised way. In *Fire Walk With Me* the whole nail is torn off, raw, covered in dead flesh, and the sound crackles and squelches as the camera gets right into the exposed digit. Even though the TV scenes are uncomfortable to watch they could never have had this level of visceral intensity. But whenever freedoms are gained others are sacrificed. The weekly format of the television series gave Lynch the opportunity to explore a broad canvas – a large cast, intertwined relationships and slowly developing plotlines that wove in and out as the programme progressed. The concerns of cinema distributors – the longer the film, the less commercially viable – generally restricts a feature film's allowable running time. Depending on various media reports, the original cut of *Fire Walk With Me* was anywhere between four and six hours long – far more than would be acceptable to cinema chains. Consequently, the languid pace and many of the show's most popular characters were either sidelined or axed entirely to keep the film to a more manageable length. Sometimes this was also down to necessity.

Sherilyn Fenn was unavailable to reprise her role as Audrey, hence the whole Horne family are absent with only a passing reference to Johnny remaining. Also missing are Ed and Nadine, Pete and Catherine and the entire Twin Peaks police department. Bizarrely, Heidi, the giggling waitress of the Double R Diner, is actually present. More problematic for the script was Kyle MacLachlan's reluctance to return as Dale Cooper for fear of being typecast. Eventually he agreed on condition that the role was substantially reduced. Much of the material was rewritten and the character of Agent Chester Desmond created to cover parts of the inquiry that couldn't be removed from the script.

On the surface *Fire Walk With Me* is a simplistic film that really offers nothing new to the series' audience, fleshing out details that were already common knowledge. Laura herself, the focus for the series and its epicentre, was never seen alive in the programme except in a grainy video taken by James. Her dead, blue face was the image that sold the series. The film's tag-line, 'These are the last seven days of Laura Palmer', pretty much tells the audience what they are to expect. With this in mind it seems that there is nothing left to surprise people – there is no mystery. We know Laura is going to die, where she is going to die and even at whose hands. What, ultimately, is the point? Well, true to the series' adage, Laura is 'full of secrets' and so is the film. The events and plot may be familiar but what's important are exploring secrets, uncovering mysteries and seeing into places which are removed from our comprehension yet intersect with it. It is about the malleability of time, the state of dreaming and the darkness in the mundane.

The way the film 'explains' the character – the catalyst for a series from which she was absent – is through showing her last known movements as juxtaposed with the interventions of another plane. The film tries to tie up the loose ends of the series by fitting events into the overall *Twin Peaks* world rather than explaining them explicitly. This technique would prove invaluable to Lynch when salvaging the cancelled series *Mulholland Dr.* Similarly, the way in which time can be fashioned into a dreamlike logic, neither forward nor backward but existing simultaneously, would feed into both *Lost Highway* and *INLAND EMPIRE*. What wrongfoots the viewer of *Fire Walk With Me* is that the linear plot is so basic that extraneous information can appear to be weird for weirdness' sake. But this is not the case. Laura's dreams are real in that they have corporeal effect – the creatures from the Black Lodge and the denizens who live above the convenience store manifest themselves as entities that affect the 'real' world. *Fire Walk With Me* is just as much a film about relating this other world to our own as it is about Laura's last week.

By and large aficionados felt that the abrupt ending of *Twin Peaks* did not provide a satisfactory conclusion. *Fire Walk With Me* goes some way towards making amends, allowing a resolution that encompasses the whole series and its main two characters (Dale and Laura), as well as offering what appears to be the final explanation of Cooper's cryptic dream. It is an ending as paradoxically uplifting and hopeful as it is apocalyptic and depressing. As we know, Lynch often offers redemptive, even angelic, endings but perhaps none are so encompassing or extreme as this one. Due to the way that time is fractured we can ascertain that the evil Cooper who escaped the lodge at the close of the series is here to stay – the bloodied Annie reveals as much to Laura –

and that the good Cooper is trapped. Cooper will grow old in the Black Lodge; he has moved to another world, trapped in a Möbius strip time structure that will similarly engulf Fred Madison in *Lost Highway*. Cooper's dream has finally been revealed, not so much a vision but more a shift in time and space. Laura Palmer is dead, murdered by her father. Not the most uplifting of endings but one that is paradoxically hopeful. Laura is seen laughing, free of the burden of life, reaching a sense of enlightenment with Cooper as they are blessed by an angel. This is the angel that had disappeared from Laura's bedside picture, only to appear in the flesh to herald her ascent to a higher, better state of consciousness.

With the denizens of the Black Lodge, Lynch consolidated and expanded the pantheon of characters from the other worlds that populate his films. This group of oddities would continue to grow in the worlds of *Lost Highway* and *Mulholland Dr.* They are, in some ways, children of *Eraserhead*'s Man in the Planet. Residing in the convenience store portal between our world and the Black Lodge, Mike and Bob share their space with a menagerie of grotesque misfits. It's revealed that The Man from Another Place is Mike The One Armed Man's hacked off limb. Mrs Tremond (Chalfont) and her grandson are also creatures of this place, implied but never explicitly stated elsewhere. They exist in the crackles of electricity that surge through the film, affecting the airwaves and claiming Officer Jeffries for their own. Electricity is the lifeblood of the film, the chaos in which the other state dwells. It makes up the video snow that starts the film and pulses irregularly as a portent of bad things.

'With this ring I thee wed,' announces the Man from Another Place. In *Fire Walk With Me* the jade owl ring ties everything together; it is prominent on the hand of the angry One Armed Man as he castigates Leland in front of Laura. This forces Leland temporarily to remember events the year before, when on a business trip he slept with Teresa Banks. Banks possessed the same ring, the ring that would become the focus for Bob/Leland during his killing time. The ring would ultimately mark Laura and not Ronette as Bob's next victim. From inside the lodge the good Cooper begs her, 'Don't take the ring Laura'. This ring first becomes significant because of its absence from Teresa's body when examined by Chester and Sam – it proves to be 'not what it seems' and marks a victim, like the rune in MR James's *Casting of the Runes*. Much more is made of the relationship between Ronette, Laura and Teresa Banks. The series gave the impression that the only link to Teresa was through her killer. However, Teresa worked as a prostitute at the same time as Laura and Ronette. In fact we are shown that Leland's penchant for visiting prostitutes on business trips almost led to him paying to sleep with his own daughter. Laura's other life, with Ronette, shows that Teresa Banks was far more connected to Twin Peaks than we had been led to believe.

The catalyst for the TV series was the discovery of Laura's body and the repercussions of her life. *Fire Walk With Me* is a microcosm of the series with the body of Teresa Banks acting as its catalyst. Teresa's influence spreads beyond the time of her death much as Laura's did in the series. Indeed much of the opening quarter of the film, which initially seems nothing but a distraction, feeds into the end of Laura's life, either as a foreshadowing of the series or through its use of puzzles and mysteries. Lynch would later employ this non-linear time structure and the intertwined stories to contrast the different lives of Nikki/Susan in *INLAND EMPIRE*.

An occasionally frustrating experience, *Twin Peaks: Fire Walk With Me* rewards repeat viewings with ever more realised detail and subtlety. Beneath the broad brushstrokes of its basic narrative lies a labyrinth of mysteries and secrets – such stuff as dreams are made on. Like the owls, it's not what it seems.

SO WHAT DID THE FISH TELL YOU?

When *Fire Walk With Me* received a mauling from the critics, Lynch took a step back from the world of feature films and started working on a number of smaller projects.

On the Air (1992)

Created by: Mark Frost and David Lynch
Directed by: Jack Fisk, Mark Frost, Lesli Linka Glatter, David Lynch, Jonathan Sanger, Betty Thomas
Cast: Ian Buchanan (Lester Guy), Nancye Ferguson (Ruth Trueworthy), Miguel Ferrer (Buddy Budwaller), Gary Grossman (Bert Schein), Mel Johnson Jr (Mickey), Marvin Kaplan (Dwight McGonigle), David L Lander (Gochktch), Kim McGuire (Nicole Thorne), Marla Rubinoff (Betty Hudson), Tracey Walter (Blinky Watts), Buddy Douglas (Buddy Morris)

1957 and The Lester Guy Show is on the air as part of ZBC (Zoblotnik Broadcasting Corporation), in association with Wellbee Snaps Dogfood. 'If it's powder they'll bark louder!' But the studio is getting tense as the debut show approaches: leading lady Betty is worried about the ironing, the Wellbee Snaps dog needs encouragement to eat on cue and Lester is still perfecting his avant-garde dancing technique. Director Gochktch still needs to find the correct end of a megaphone to bark down and studio executive Buddy Budwaller is causing nerves all around with his threats from above. What could possibly go right?

Aside from *Twin Peaks*, Lynch and Frost's creative collaborations had led to a number of unrealised screenplays. One of these, *One Saliva Bubble*, was a totally absurd comedy that played on notions of slap-stick, wordplay and repetition, the spirit of which was borne out on the small screen in the form of *On the Air*. Reuniting some of the members of *Twin Peaks* along with newcomers and the occasional cult figure – Freddie Jones plays a wheezing, gesticulating English stage actor while Kim McGuire provides a suitably sneering sidekick to Miguel Ferrer's caustic Buddy Budwaller – *On the Air* was an apparently anarchic yet tightly honed character comedy that bemused as much as it amused. It made full use of the cause and effect logic of *One Saliva Bubble*, the conclusion of each episode almost inevitably resulting in the humiliation of self-absorbed Lester in front of an audience of millions. The real star of the show, Betty, is so naïve (half way between Betty in *Mulholland Dr.* and Lucy from *Twin Peaks*) that she is oblivious of all the plotting to oust her from her position as audience favourite, a position gained by rescuing the disastrous opening show with a saccharine song. Every episode is populated with regular characters that round out the produc-tion – the Hurry-Up Twins (jogging conjoined twins who chant 'hurry up'), Blinky the soundman (whose Bozeman's Simplex condition results in him seeing 25.6 times as much as anyone else – rendering him virtu-ally blind) and occasional characters like ventriloquist dummy Mr Peanuts. The director, Gochktch, speaks in an outrageous European accent and mixes his vowels so badly he's in need of constant transla-tion.

Lynch wrote and directed the opening show and co-wrote the final episode in this constantly entertaining series. But sadly *On the Air*'s fabulous cast, zany humour (*Hellzapoppin'* meets *Monty Python's Flying Circus*) and quality production values came to nothing. The show was quickly axed in the USA – of the seven produced only three were ever aired, while in the UK it only ran post-midnight on BBC2. A brief run on video did little to revive the show's fortunes and it has remained one of Lynch's least seen works. It is a shame because *On the Air* broke the tedious predictability of the 22-minute studio based sitcom, a genre Lynch would later mercilessly parody in *Rabbits*. It seemed to many that the programme was designed specifically to antagonise; the gags were too dense, too fast, too puerile, too clever or just too stupid. The slapstick crowd couldn't cope with the intellectual nature of the plot with its complex relationships and warped scenarios. The *Twin Peaks* crowd couldn't handle the breakneck pace and the reliance on schoolboy 'fart gag' toilet humour. Everyone else just didn't care. *On the Air* was a brave and enjoyable programme showcasing aspects of absurdist comedy often ignored in Lynch's other work by bringing them out into the open. Ultimately, however, it was a further indication of the critical backlash that was brewing following the demise of *Twin Peaks*.

Hotel Room (1993)

Directed by: David Lynch (*Tricks, Blackout*), James Signorelli (*Getting Rid of Robby*)
Written by: Barry Gifford (*Tricks, Blackout*), Jay McInerney (*Getting Rid of Robby*)
Produced by: Deepak Nayer, (exec) David Lynch & Monty Montgomery
Cast: Clark Heathcliffe Brolly (Bellboy), Freddie Jones (Louis), Harry Dean Stanton (Moe Boca), Glenne Headly (Darlene), Crispin Glover (Danny), Alicia Witt (Diane)

'For a millennium the space for the hotel room existed, undefined. Mankind captured it, gave it shape and passed through. And sometimes in passing through they found themselves brushing up against the secret names of truth.'

Tricks (1969): Boca and Darlene, a prostitute, are shown to their hotel room. Boca is agitated and orders a Scotch while Darlene smokes a joint. Boca's acquaintance Lou arrives and starts to dominate proceedings. After swapping anecdotes about Lou's first wife, Felicia, Lou has sex with Darlene. Boca reveals that Felicia is really his wife. Darlene leaves the weirdoes, and Lou soon departs, leaving Boca to be arrested by the police for Felicia's murder. It turns out his real name is Lou.

Blackout (1936): Danny's return to the room with some Chinese food for his confused wife, Diane, is not made any easier by a power cut. They are in the city to see a doctor about her condition. Diane tells Danny about her dream of the Chinese fortune-telling fish and their six children. Twelve years earlier their son had drowned at the age of two in Lake Osage and the repercussions are still being felt. At least while the blackout lasts.

Originally conceived by David Lynch and Monty Montgomery as a television series, *Hotel Room* offered a combination of flexibility and familiarity in its novel premise. Each story would take place in a single New York hotel room – room 603. The only other locations permissible were the corridor outside the room and the hotel lobby. The only characters that would remain consistent from one story to the next were the bellboy and the maid. Within these parameters any writer on the show would be given free reign, the sole remit being the year that the story was to take place. An elegant premise for a half hour show. Unlike Lynch's previous foray into the world of television, *Hotel Room* was planned to broadcast on the cable network HBO, a subscription channel significantly less censorious than its terrestrial counterparts, allowing greater freedom for expression.

Following the success of *Wild at Heart*, Lynch was keen to work with Barry Gifford and approached him to write three scripts for the series. One should be something that Lynch and co-producer Monty Montgomery's 'grandmothers could watch'. No problem, said the writer, 'I'll write the play, you guys gag and tie up the old ladies'.[15] Of the three scripts produced by Gifford only two, *Tricks* and *Blackout*, were made, both directed by David Lynch. The third, *Mrs Kashfi*, was deemed too controversial, even for HBO, because it featured a young boy and an older woman. A further instalment of the series, *Getting Rid of Robby*, was written by Jay McInerney and directed by James Signorelli. They were the only three episodes produced. The series was shelved, despite gaining good ratings when they were originally broadcast. Lynch's contributions, however, were initially shortened to fit the scheduled running times.

Hotel Room's opening sequence of industrialisation gives way to shots of superimposed people, a style that would provide the genesis of the opening of *Mulholland Dr.* Angelo Badalamenti's languid score, rich in strings, sets the pace for this series of parlour plays, self-contained mini-dramas boxed in by the four walls of the hotel room. The sense of claustrophobia that the deliberately limited setting imposes on the productions forces us to concentrate on the characters and the actors who portray them. These are primarily actors' pieces but, as with *Eraserhead*, Lynch makes use of the confined space to link the characters to their surroundings. The fluid camerawork makes plenty of the art-deco hotel corridor, complete with Lynch's familiar upward-pointing lamps and its textures of wood and metal. In *Tricks* the duality of the characters, or at least their deliberate identity confusion, can be seen as a precursor to the more elaborate characterisations of *Lost Highway* and *Mulholland Dr.* A couple's psychoanalytic deconstruction of a dream, *Blackout* is even more intimate, effectively a two-person drama. Diane's guilt at their son's death, her possible involvement and her subsequent sexual repression all make for difficult viewing. Its claustrophobia is heightened by tight, imposing candlelight that picks out parts of the frame. Diane is in the dark in both senses of the word; her world blurs reality and dreamtime in a way that appears to offer only superficial hope. The final shot of the couple bathed in the glorious electric light may seem like an uplifting climax but it feels as artificial as the robin at the close of *Blue Velvet*.

Lumière and Company: Premonitions Following an Evil Deed (Lumière et compagnie) (1995)

Directed by: David Lynch
Produced by: Neil Edelstein
Edited by: Mary Sweeney
Cinematography: Peter Deming
Music: David Lynch and Angelo Badalamenti

A body is discovered by the police. Some women clad in white are troubled. A vision appears of a floating, naked woman suspended in glass, struggling, and being tormented by bestial creatures. The frame burns through to reveal a family awaiting bad news.

In an inspired piece of prime concept marketing some of the world's most internationally regarded directors were invited to produce a short film. Of the 150 or so approached, 40 agreed to the proposition. The request came with strings attached – no synch sound, natural light, a single shot, length less than a minute, a maximum of three takes to get that shot and, most importantly, the film had to be made using a very special camera. That camera was the one used by the Lumière brothers themselves in 1895 at the very birth of cinema. Lovingly restored by Philippe Poulet of Lyon's Musée du Cinéma, whose idea sparked the project, the camera was supplied with replica film stock (he even had the original formula for the emulsion, but omitted the nitrate for reasons of safety) featuring just one sprocket hole per frame. The small square, mainly wooden, box was to be operated by hand crank. Truly a global film, David Lynch was to find himself in the company, albeit by association, of such diverse directors as Bigas Luna, Peter Greenaway, Wim Wenders, Abbas Kiarostami and Yimou Zhang.

It's not difficult to see why Lynch would have been so intrigued by the project, especially as it was linked to cinema's inception. The nature of the camera led to flickering images due to the way the shutter worked.

The film itself was grainy, organic and otherworldly and the hand-cranked operation meant that the human element altered apparent time at a subconscious level. The restrictions put the filmmaker on a par with cinema's forefathers and presented a challenge to examine new ways of using old technology. The advantage the modern filmmaker had over his forebears was that cinema language had been defined in the intervening hundred years through exposure and assimilation; for the earliest camera operators this was a process of trial and error.

Lynch's offering to the project was *Premonitions Following an Evil Deed*, probably the most bizarre 55 seconds of film you are likely to see. It is made even more intriguing when you try and figure out how the film was actually made – the film cuts between several locations in its short running time but we are aware that the conditions of the filming required it to be shot in a single take. 'Once you start the cranking, you couldn't stop.'[16] Logistically the staging of events had to be precise and intricately rehearsed. The lack of synch sound allows for some leeway and off-screen direction but even so this is a remarkable achievement, the space between each shot achieved by simply blocking the light to the camera, deliberately overexposing the film to hide a transition or, in one change-over, being achieved by a burning curtain revealing another scene behind it, apparently separated in time and space. All the while the soundtrack plays mood music punctuated with the regular pulse of a record that has reached the end of its groove.

FUNNY HOW TIME SLIPS AWAY

Having been involved with a number of small-scale projects, including some that never reached fruition, Lynch was keen to get back into the world of feature films. *Lost Highway* was the next in his deal with CiBy 2000 and saw him teaming up once again with writer Barry Gifford. Up until this point, their relationship had been hands-off – Lynch had worked on the script for *Wild At Heart* himself and been content to go with Gifford's script for *Hotel Room* – but this time they would write together.

Lost Highway (1997)

Directed by: David Lynch
Written by: David Lynch & Barry Gifford
Produced by: Deepak Nayar, Tom Sternberg, Mary Sweeney
Edited by: Mary Sweeney
Cinematography: Peter Deming
Music: Angelo Badalamenti
Cast: Bill Pullman (Fred Madison), Patricia Arquette (Renee Madison/ Alice Wakefield), Balthazar Getty (Pete Dayton), Robert Loggia (Dick Laurent/Mr Eddy), Jack Nance (Phil), John Roselius (Al), Louis Eppolito (Ed), Michael Massee (Andy), Robert Blake (Mystery Man), Henry Rollins (Guard Henry), Mink Stole (Forewoman), Gary Busey (Bill Dayton), Lucy Butler (Candace Dayton), Richard Pryor (Arnie)

Saxophonist Fred Madison receives a message that Dick Laurent is dead. After a particularly raucous gig one evening, he phones his wife Renee at home, but is confused to find that she doesn't answer his call. The next morning they find a mysterious package on their doorstep containing video footage of their home. More tapes arrive, showing the interior of the house and even shots of them in bed together. Worried about this invasion of privacy, Fred and Renee alert the police.

At a party held by Renee's friend Andy, Fred meets the Mystery Man, who can apparently answer the phone at Fred's house, even as he stands right in front of him. Andy tells Fred that the strange guy is a friend of Dick Laurent. Back home, a new videotape has arrived and Fred watches it alone. To his horror, it contains shots of him killing Renee.

Found guilty of murder, he is sentenced to death and locked up. The next morning the guards are shocked to find that their prisoner is not Fred. He is Pete Dayton, a very confused mechanic. His worried parents collect him and detectives follow them to discover why he ended up in the cell.

Pete returns to work and is immediately called upon by Mr Eddy. They go out for a drive so that Pete can retune the Mercedes but are hassled by a tailgater. Mr Eddy waves for him to overtake, then rams the car from behind and attacks the driver. Thanking Pete for his efforts, Mr Eddy offers him a porno. Next day he brings the Caddy to the garage and Pete becomes captivated by the beautiful passenger, Alice. That evening Alice invites Pete to dinner and they begin a secret liaison. Alice begins to fear that Mr Eddy suspects her infidelity and hatches a plan to steal some money from a friend so that she and Pete can leave. On arrival at her friend Andy's apartment, Pete sees a porno film starring Alice. Pete kills Andy and the pair escape. Arriving at a cabin in the desert, Alice seduces Pete then drops him flat. 'You will never have me.' Fred follows Alice into the cabin and finds the Mystery Man, who tells him that her name is, in fact, Renee. The Mystery Man and Fred both kill Mr Eddy at the cabin. Fred drives off in his car, hotly pursued by the police.

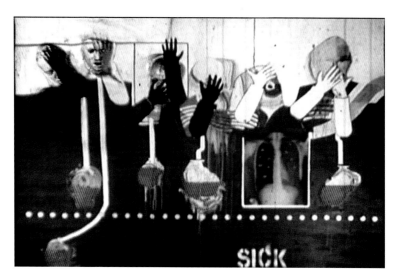

Six Figures Getting Sick.

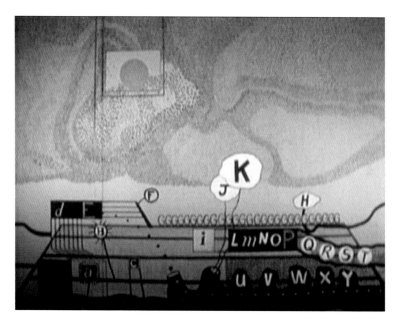

The Alphabet. Learning ABCs the David Lynch way.

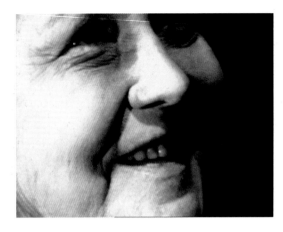

Pasty-faced adoration from *The Grandmother*.

David Lynch discusses the Elephant Man's tumultuous return to London with John Hurt.

Moving Pictures: Betty (Naomi Watts) and Rita (Laura Elena Harring) watch the show at the Silencio Club

The baroque spaceship of Dune's Guild Navigators.

Kyle MacLachlan delivers an ultimatum in *Dune*.

Role reversal. Isabella Rossellini gets dominant in *Blue Velvet*.

Another diner moment as David Lynch directs Laura Dern in *Blue Velvet*.

The Blue Lady (Isabella Rossellini) and the Blue Pianist (Angelo Badalamenti) play *Blue Velvet*.

Laura Dern in *INLAND EMPIRE*. A woman in love and in trouble. Studio Canal.

Sailor (Nicolas Cage) and Lula (Laura Dern) prepare to hit the town in *Wild at Heart*. Rockin' good!

Lipstick and lunacy from Diane Ladd in *Wild at Heart*.

The Straight Story – Alvin (Richard Farnsworth) finds himself coming last in a bicycle race.

Nicolas Cage and David Lynch share a joke on the set of *Wild at Heart*. Samuel Goldwyn Company/Photofest.

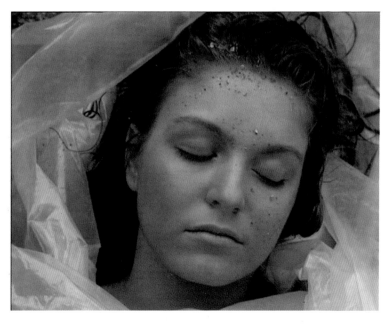

Twin Peaks' grim discovery – Laura Palmer (Sheryl Lee). Dead. Wrapped in plastic.

Red Curtains in the Black Lodge – the Man From Another Place (Michael J Anderson) directs Agent Cooper's (Kyle MacLachlan) attention in *Fire Walk With Me*. Photofest.

Betty (Naomi Watts) dreaming of sunny palm trees and Hollywood in *Mulholland Dr.* Universal Focus/Photofest.

Looking red, feeling blue – Fred Madison (Bill Pullman) finds himself starting out on the Lost Highway. October Films/Photofest.

Let's Roque! David Lynch and Michael J Anderson discuss Roque's role in *Mulholland Dr.* Universal Focus/Photofest.

Lost Highway is the middle segment in Lynch's loose trilogy of films deconstructing the road movie. By their very nature road movies are about direction, about going somewhere. Often this is as much a psychological journey as a physical one – finding oneself on the road or forming a relationship. *Wild at Heart* tells the story of Sailor and Lula, how they redefine their relationship following estrangement and the journey from being a couple to becoming a family. In *The Straight Story* Alvin's expedition is more than physical, it is about reconciliation. *Lost Highway* differs in that its existential voyage ultimately leads to where it began – a never-ending journey of despair forever accelerating but never escaping its confines. Fred's desperate need to find the truth creates such a rift in his psyche that he is ultimately doomed – Prometheus-like – to relive the same fate for all eternity. Most highways have a beginning and an end but *Lost Highway* has neither; it is a Möbius strip of a film, infinite yet bound.

As a road movie *Lost Highway* has a great deal to do with the process of driving and the maintenance of machinery, a trait it shares with *The Straight Story*. Pete's profession is car related too: he is a mechanic. Arguably it is the link between cars, their drivers and their mechanics that draws Pete in to Mr Eddy's murky world. Other Lynchian mechanics (Big Ed or the twins from *The Straight Story*) remain rooted to where they work, needing to remain stationary to allow other people to travel. Pete makes the mistake (although it's his job) of getting into a car with Mr Eddy and, as Jeffrey Beaumont found in *Blue Velvet*, riding with a dangerous man leads to dangerous consequences. Some filmmakers fetishise cars but Lynch is fascinated with machinery in general. Although *Lost Highway* begins and concludes with the sense of speed on the road, it's the full driving experience, the link between man and machine that appeals, not simply the exhilaration of acceleration. In this way there is no real difference between Mr Eddy's Mercedes, Alvin Straight's John Deere riding mower or the spice collectors of Arrakis – all are of a mechanical interest rather than an outlet for testosterone (*Fast and the Furious*), worship (*Scorpio Rising*) or nostalgia (*American Graffiti*). Curiously, although Fred/Pete ends up driving at breakneck speed, the real danger in driving is shown when Mr Eddy tries to enjoy his leisurely paced cruise down Mulholland Dr. only to be tailgated. Both the tailgater and Mr Eddy drive irresponsibly, but Mr Eddy forces the man off the road and confronts him in a manner at once understandable, funny and very frightening. It also shows how something that we take for granted is but a hair's breadth away from being deadly – we have seen the aftermath of the crashes in *Wild at Heart* and in the opening of *Mulholland Dr.*

As a film *Lost Highway* asks far more questions than it answers, but unlike *Mulholland Dr.* it contains fewer overtly surreal events. Fred/Pete's predicament, however fanciful or preposterous, is nonetheless tinged with an air of plausibility. It is the individual characters that provide the sense of surrealism here. The film is grounded in the realms of reality, albeit a sleazy one, that the viewer, like Fred, would rather not confront. Perhaps the initial confusion occurs when Fred transmogrifies into Pete – an event that can be viewed either literally or as some sort of psychologically induced schism from a man on the verge of execution. The change comes about almost without provocation. In the original screenplay far more attention was given to the capture and trial of Fred along with his increasing headaches that go some way to explaining his change in psychological and perhaps physical state. But the real enigma of the film is the spooky pasty-faced Mystery Man, who could be perpetrating the crimes. There is also an implication that Fred may be the Mystery Man, either directly or by association. Fred ends up killing those he feels have let him down. Is the Mystery Man a persona onto which he can offload his guilt? But then this is assuming that Fred is responsible for the murder of his wife. He may well be an innocent man. On the one hand, you can view his transformation as a way of freeing a man wrongly accused, or you could assume that he is escaping from reality. As the Mystery Man says to Pete, 'In the East... when a person is sentenced to death... they are sent to a far place never knowing when an executioner will step up behind them and fire a bullet into the back of their head. It could be days... weeks... or even years after the death sentence has been pronounced'.

Themes of voyeurism abound in Lynch's work, from the desire to see the 'terrible' Elephant Man to Jeffrey's escapades in Dorothy's closet, but *Lost Highway* extends its voyeurism into the realm of the technical and in doing so seeks to question the audience's desire to watch without consequences. Fred is paranoid about surveillance and has every right to be. His home, his sanctuary, is being penetrated deeper each night by an unseen person who films Fred and Renee while they sleep. When they receive the tapes they effectively become voyeurs of themselves. The connection between these events and Pete's experiences is also via video. Pete is offered porno by Mr Eddy but, like Fred, he doesn't want to watch an 'uninvited' tape. Ultimately he has no choice. When Pete breaks into Andy's house to get 'easy money' he sees Alice in a porno film projected large on the wall. Later we learn that these porno films go a little harder than most as it is revealed that they could be porno snuff flicks.

Pete/Fred's introduction to this world is through the Mystery Man (a precursor in some ways to *Mulholland Dr.'s* Cowboy), himself seen with a camera glued to his right eye, the ultimate voyeur. *Lost Highway* offers a comment on the difference between film and video. It is shot on luscious 35mm film stock and in 2.35:1 Panavision format, but the invasion of the moving image into people's homes as shown in *Lost Highway* is through the medium of video or lower definition film. Lynch himself would eventually take to video as a means of expression by using normal definition cameras to produce short experimental work such as *Darkened Room* or *Rabbits*. The technical shortcomings of the medium are offset by its immediacy and its universality. 35mm film production requires big bankrolls and experienced technicians while video can democratise work, allowing people to express ideas otherwise impossible under the studio system. This universality is also its downfall, and *Lost Highway* shows that the ubiquity of the electronic image has implications for personal privacy and a greater freedom to exploit others with impunity. The very fact that video is electronic means that the chaos in the wires can manifest itself in the subtle variations on a monitor screen. This ultimately sees fruition in the 'film' *INLAND EMPIRE*, shot entirely on digital video to give it an immediacy that relates to audiences' own experience of the medium whilst also allowing the textured electronic chaos to invade the screen space.

Lost Highway shows a complementary side to the film industry that's depicted in *Mulholland Dr.*, around whose snaking road both films are based. Betty's world is one where the dream factory is alive and well – pushing morally appropriate entertainment to the masses. It is a world of glamour, where stardom is ultimately more important than financial gain, a day-glo amalgam of daytime dramas and *On the Air* style variety shows. But, as we know, the mundane, happy, wholesome side of apple-pie munching American life has a darker side that lurks in the shadows. The American pornographic film industry is one of the largest and most profitable in the world, in some areas outstripping Hollywood product in terms of sheer turnover. *Mulholland Dr.* started as a television pilot, in a medium where sex and foul language are not tolerated. *Lost Highway*, whilst still falling under the auspices of the MPAA, shows the other side. It's this contradiction that is so fascinating – a culture where one exposed nipple creates a national scandal in a country that consumes enormous amounts of hardcore pornography. *Lost Highway* shows the seedier side of even the porno industry. Mr Eddy's manner of coercing his actresses is not pleasant as he forces them to strip and fellate him at gunpoint in front of a roomful of strangers. They are then compelled to star in increasingly dark films, culminating in orgies of sexual degradation, designed to arouse Mr Eddy's need for ever more extreme pornography.

Lost Highway was a very musical production, and writers Lynch and Gifford had spent some time researching the music beforehand. The script describes particular songs for inclusion, which often relate directly to events. The diversity of the soundtrack enhances the visual richness of the film. Angelo Badalamenti's screeching saxophones contrast with Barry Adamson's evocatively sleazy *Mr Eddy's Theme*, while the metal-industrial nihilism of Rammstein adds an uncomfortable but overblown edge. The excellent sound is not just the result of the score, of course; the film rumbles as only a Lynch film can, with moments of eerie quiet giving way to monumentally loud rushes of sound. If you see this in the cinema, insist that they turn up the volume to ear bleeding levels and live with the consequences later.

I WANT TO SIT WITH HIM, LOOK UP AT THE STARS

It sounds like an unlikely pitch: a wholesome, feel-good, life-affirming film from Walt Disney brought to the screen by the man who gave you *Eraserhead* and *Lost Highway*. On the surface it would appear that *The Straight Story*, the David Lynch film for all the family, is a passing oddity in his canon but in reality it bears all the hallmarks of his other work, especially the power of redemptive love and the existence of the absurd in the apparently mundane.

The Straight Story (1999)

Directed by: David Lynch
Written by: Mary Sweeney, John Roach
Produced by: Mary Sweeney, Neil Edelstein
Edited by: Mary Sweeney
Cinematography: Freddie Francis
Music: Angelo Badalamenti
Cast: Richard Farnsworth (Alvin Straight), Sissy Spacek (Rose), Jane Galloway Heitz (Dorothy), Everett McGill (Tom the Dealer), John Farley (Thorvald), Kevin P Farley (Harald), John Lordan (Priest), Harry Dean Stanton (Lyle), Anastasia Webb (Crystal), Matt Guidry (Steve), Bill McCallum (Rat), Barbara Robertson (Deer Woman), Wiley Harker (Verlyn Heller)

Laurens, Iowa. Alvin Straight, a frail old man who walks using sticks, lives with his daughter Rose. One night, during a raging thunderstorm, Alvin discovers that his estranged brother Lyle has suffered a stroke. Determined to patch up their relationship, Alvin decides to visit him. The trouble is, Lyle lives over 300 miles away in Mount Zion, Wisconsin, and 73-year-old Alvin is legally unable to drive a car due to his poor eyesight. Undaunted he hatches a plan. He will ride his Rhoda lawnmower all the way to Lyle. Sadly the Rhoda is not up to the task and splutters to a halt outside Grotto. Reunited prematurely with his daughter, Alvin's stubbornness knows no bounds, so he approaches Tom the Dealer to fix him up with a new vehicle, a '66 John Deere riding lawnmower from Tom's personal collection. Setting off once more, Alvin's epic but leisurely journey sees him reuniting a runaway hitchhiker with her family, coming last in a bicycle race and encountering a woman who inadvertently kills deer. As the landscape begins to undulate, his trusty mower goes out of control with fan-belt and transmission failure. Alvin gets his steed repaired and sets off again, crossing the Mississippi and slowly approaching his brother's home. After drinking his first beer in years, Alvin makes the final stage of the journey to be reunited with his brother.

The Straight Story is the final film in Lynch's 'road movie' trilogy, retaining the genre's format but slowing events down to a septuagenarian pace; the promise of the open road and freedom remain but at a speed where every stone on the road tells its own story. *The Straight Story* is an unusual film in that there is no conflict and little threat. The only things that stand in the way of Alvin completing his monumental journey are himself and the elements of chance. His journey is a spiritual one, a personal pilgrimage. He is not simply reconciling with his estranged brother, he is discovering himself. On the long road, Alvin finally has time to think about who he really is and what his life means. It is as much a metaphysical journey as a physical one. And it is only when he opens up to total strangers, outside his normal community, that he can confront his past and begin to put everything into a broader context. This is a cleansing process that prepares him for his emotional reunion with his brother – estranged for so long over an incident that neither of them can recall. Their mutual parting of ways shows that stubbornness – seen as a virtue in Alvin's gritty determination to 'finish this one my own way' – can also be a self-made barrier to the love between brothers. Alvin's realisation of his own failings allows him the chance to repent. His recollection of his alcoholism and the accidental shooting of a scout during the war are confessions that lift a burden from his shoulders. He goes to his brother a new and cleansed man, reconciled as much with the world and himself as with his brother.

The Straight Story forces us to look at the world with different eyes. Road movies usually contain sequences of low-angled roads, cars shooting off into the distance and the blur of road markings. The contrast here reflects the slower pace of Alvin's life, his mode of transport and the gentle winding down of old age. When Alvin takes to the road there are no speed blurs in the paint lines, instead every detail can be seen trundling along at a sedate, considered rate. When the camera slowly cranes up from the mower and trailer combination we see the vast and beautiful expanse of the American plains stretching out to the horizon in the morning sun. Lynch holds this shot to take in the splendour before slowly craning back down to find that Alvin has progressed very little in the time. The only occasion on which Alvin reaches double figures on the speedometer is when his John Deere finally develops a fault. Unable to apply the brakes, Alvin and his vehicle keep gaining momentum as they career down a hill, in front of a group of firemen hosing down a house deliberately set alight for them to test their skills (in real life there was such a fire on Alvin's journey). The residents of the little town watch in disbelief as he hurtles past them.

The story's central conceit is so bizarre and seemingly contrived that the viewer knows it must be true. It's another example of the absurd that can be found within the ordinary. The celebration of the diversity and strangeness in the lives of ordinary Americans is perhaps best served in the documentary series that Lynch produced, *American Chronicles*, which took a gentle look at the quirkier side of life in a travelogue format. Here, too, Alvin's travel leads to several encounters that are plausible yet bizarre, especially when added to the hunched figure trundling along, silhouetted against the open road. Often it's the juxtaposition that creates the absurdity. An old man telling a runaway pregnant girl the value of family seems like a standard morality lecture, although he too is coming to terms with his own estrangement. What makes it less sanctimonious is Alvin's straight talking earnestness – 'Eat your dinner missy' – and the fact that he encountered the girl hitchhiking. In the fast-paced world of the car a hitchhiker is either a quick stop or quickly forgot, but here she watches him slowly passing by. Similarly the cycle racers provide us with humour, as vehicles usually overtake bikes. In the film's most bizarre scene a car overtakes Alvin at great speed only to crash into a deer. The driver is distraught; this happens to her on a regular basis on the only route to and from work. There's humour in the scene but also a message: life lived at a fast pace doesn't necessarily get you anywhere more quickly. The woman is so tied up in her own life she needs to travel from the fold of her cosy town to live a big city dream, shown here as a poor choice compared to the slow, stately ideal of small town living. Alvin's response to this is practical – he ends up with a hearty meal of venison and some trophy antlers to mount on his trailer.

Rather like *The Elephant Man*, *The Straight Story* is based on fact. Lynch's partner Mary Sweeney had been attracted to the story when it featured on the news and tried to buy the filming rights, only to find they had already been taken. As soon as the option lapsed she snapped it up and began to work on the screenplay. Showing the script to Lynch for his opinion she was shocked to find that he liked the story so much that he wanted to direct it. The screenplay necessarily alters some of the actuality – the focus is not so much about portraying the reality of life, but rather its feelings. It is impossible accurately to compress six weeks into two hours and little purpose is gained in showing details that alter the simple emotional depth of the story. What is true is that 73-year-old Alvin Straight travelled from Laurens, Iowa, to Mount Zion in Wisconsin in 1994 to see his ailing brother and patch up their differences in the twilight of their lives. He rode a 1966 John Deere lawnmower on an epic six-week journey, having several adventures along the way. Legally blind and suffering from arthritis, his journey is testament to the man's stubborn determination. One incident that didn't make the film, however, was Straight's brush with the law in New Hampton for causing a massive traffic jam. Such a scene would have completely unbalanced a film whose message is as direct as the protagonist's name.

Alvin meets bemusement on his travels but never hostility; this is a film that celebrates the diversity of people but also the natural humanity in us all. President of Walt Disney Motion Picture Group Peter Schneider said, 'It's a beautiful movie about values, forgiveness and healing, and celebrates America'. If this statement sounds saccharine or trite, within this context it shouldn't. *The Straight Story*'s Alvin is universal. He has failings but shows that humanity can triumph and that redemption is possible. What is more specific is the film's unashamed laudation of some of America's quieter states. This is an America far removed from the fast-talking smart-lipped yuppies in their penthouse apartments or gun-toting gangstas in ghettos. The pace of Alvin's journey, though exaggerated, reflects the pace of the states he passes through – no pimped-up boy racers, more towns where 'an amber light means slow down, not speed up'. Even the Iowa residents' assertion that Wisconsin is 'a real party state' doesn't hold up to scrutiny – it seems like the party consists of two blokes at either end of a long bar. Instead of urban sprawl, *The Straight Story* gives us luscious fields of golden soya and corn undulating in the breeze. Flat plains slowly metamorphose into rolling hills of deciduous trees turning to autumnal splendour under a deep amber sky. This is a world where machinery is devoid of its menacing aspect. Man and machine work in harmony *with* nature rather than against it. There are no choking industrial developments – here the largest of machines, harvesters and massive tractors, are put to agricultural use. Machinery is perceived as good. It is an idealised vision but one that offers hope – industrialism isn't forcing nature out but becoming part of it. Finally we have a film that fetishises the beauty of industry and machinery without the fear of its threat.

As befits a film about the twilight years of life much of *The Straight Story* is filmed with a mature, nostalgic eye. Key to this is the central performance by Richard Farnsworth, a veteran of the silver screen, stunt rider on the chariot scene in *The Ten Commandments* (1956) and companion to *Spartacus* (1960). Aged 79, he was actually older than the real-life Alvin Straight and played the role while awaiting a hip operation, forcing him to use the two sticks, thus adding a sense of realism. This adds a poignancy and verisimilitude to a remarkably un-sentimental performance (no-nonsense lumberjack shirt and trouser costumes were designed by William Zacha, a sprightly 68). The film's final moments are unbearably moving, heightened immeasurably by the weathered looks and barely contained emotions of Harry Dean Stanton, himself in his mid-70s. Stanton refused to have his name above the title because of the size of his role, and felt it was misleading to cast him among the film's stars. The film also reunited Lynch with Freddie Francis, his cinematographer on *Dune* and *Elephant Man*, who was 80 at the time. Shot in chronological order, some DVD copies deliberately have no chapter breaks, so that it must be viewed as straight as possible.

The Straight Story premiered at Cannes in 1999. This must have been the strangest festival yet for Lynch, whose film was greeted with a standing ovation from the audience, becoming the 'People's Choice'.

IT'LL BE JUST LIKE IN THE MOVIES. PRETENDING TO BE SOMEBODY ELSE.

As unlikely and triumphant a salvage job as can be imagined, *Mulholland Dr.* began life as the pilot for a television series, planned to mark Lynch's return to mainstream TV after a hiatus of nearly a decade. New television programmes are usually given a feature length pilot episode to determine audience and studio reaction to the basic premise. ABC, who were part funding the ambitious and expensive TV movie, approved the script with no changes and the pilot was shot, on time and to budget. Then the problems began. The intervening time between script approval and pilot completion had seen a marked change in attitudes about what was suitable for terrestrial broadcast, particularly when dealing with violence. *Mulholland Dr.* was one of the victims of this new Puritanism – it was too dark, too violent and too odd. It even had animal excrement in it. Not only was the planned series scrapped but the pilot would also be shelved, unaired. Having invested so much time and effort in the project Lynch was not about to let the work just fade away. He obtained additional funding from Studio Canal+ to realise an audacious plan. He would reassemble the cast and shoot an additional 45 minutes of material to make a feature film from the pilot he already had. Fortunately the pilot was shot on 35mm film. The rest is history. Rising phoenix-like from the ashes, *Mulholland Dr.* went from being a canned pilot to a Cannes winner – gaining the ultimate prize, the *Palme d'Or*.

Mulholland Dr. (2001)

Directed by: David Lynch
Written by: David Lynch
Produced by: Neal Edelstein, Tony Krantz, Michael Polaire, Joyce Eliason, Alain Sarde & Mary Sweeney
Edited by: Mary Sweeney
Cinematography: Peter Deming
Music: Angelo Badalamenti
Cast: Justin Theroux (Adam Kesher), Naomi Watts (Betty/Diane), Laura Elena Harring (Rita/Camilla), Ann Miller (Coco), Mark Pellegrino (Joe Messing), Dan Hedaya (Vincenzo Castigliane), Katharine Towne (Cynthia Jenzen), Lee Grant (Louise Bonner), Billy Ray Cyrus (Gene), Scott Coffey (Wilkins), Chad Everett (Jimmy 'Woody' Katz), Rita Taggart (Linney James), James Karen (Wally Brown), Lori Heuring (Lorraine Kesher), Angelo Badalamenti (Luigi Castigliane), Maya Bond (Aunt Ruth), Michael J Anderson (Mr Roque), Melissa George (Camilla Rhodes), Monty Montgomery (Cowboy)

Mulholland Dr., LA. Two men threaten a woman in a black Cadillac but the car is hit by a sedan full of teenage joyriders. The woman stumbles away...

Betty has arrived in LA to become an actress, staying in her Aunt Ruth's Hollywood apartment under the watchful eye of proprietor Coco. She finds a strange injured brunette who claims her name is Rita but it becomes apparent that she has no recollection of who she is; the only clues to her identity are a strange coloured key and $125,000 in her purse.

Hip film director Adam meets with the sinister Castigliane Brothers who 'persuade' him to cast Camilla Rhodes as the lead in his latest picture. Adam refuses so they shut the film down. Adam retaliates by trashing the brothers' car. Upon arriving home, he finds his wife in bed with the swimming pool man so he smothers her jewellery with pink paint and then gets roundly beaten. Covered in paint and blood, he stumbles to a motel only to find that he's broke, his credit cards withdrawn. He arranges a meeting with an intimidating cryptic Cowboy who insists he cast Camilla as the lead actress. Adam heads back to the film set to swallow his pride. The omnipotent Mr Roque observes.

Hit man Joe has had a bad day, killing half an office to get at one man. He's seeking a brunette who has disappeared recently. Meanwhile Betty and Rita try to find out Rita's identity. A chance glance at a waitress's badge at Winkies' diner reminds Rita of a name – Diane Selwyn. Looking her up in a telephone directory they phone the number. The voice on the answer-phone convinces Rita that she's not Diane.

After a particularly successful audition for Betty, she and Rita continue their investigations. They meet a woman who swapped apartments with Diane who points them in the direction of another flat. They break in and are horrified to find a rotting corpse on the bed. Rita is scared for her life but Betty comforts her. On their return home, they cement their burgeoning relationship by making love. Later, Rita wakes up and demands that Betty accompany her to the Silencio Club, where they view a surreal and tragic stage show. Upon looking in her purse, Betty finds a box, which has a lock that fits Rita's key. Back at Aunt Ruth's, Betty vanishes and Rita inserts the key into the mysterious box...

Diane Selwyn is asleep on her bed. There's a knock at the door; her apartment swap neighbour picks up her stuff. Beautiful brunette Camilla arrives and drives Diane wild with her lovemaking, before crushingly declaring that they should part. On a film set it becomes clear that Adam and Camilla are in love. Camilla takes Diane to a party on Mulholland Dr. Adam greets them and introduces his mother, Coco. The Cowboy walks past, his sinister business undetermined. Adam and Camilla announce their 'engagement', and Diane drops her coffee cup in emotional turmoil...

...as the cup tumbles Diane finds herself in Winkies' diner sitting opposite Joe. Diane produces a photo of Camilla and gives him the money from the purse. Joe confirms that she will find a blue key when the deed has been executed.

Diane finds the blue key on her coffee table. There's a knock on the door, and the old couple who travelled with Betty to LA crawl under it. Amidst laughter they attack Diane, she falls onto her bed, reaches for a gun and shoots herself. The film ends with shots of Betty and Rita superimposed on a cityscape of LA, happy and smiling.

What is so distinctive about *Mulholland Dr.* is the clear dividing line between the original pilot and the additional material. The first two-thirds of the film play like a mystery, building up an ensemble cast of characters that, one presumes, would have been fleshed out in subsequent episodes, rather as in *Twin Peaks*. Following the discovery of the body in the apartment, Rita and Betty return to Aunt Ruth's where Rita starts cutting her hair, apparently in fear of assassination. 'You look like someone else,' notes Betty. At this point the pilot ends and the new material commences. Despite the consistency of the cinematography and sound editing it's clear that this is not intended for television – the pace becomes less languid, and the language coarse, and there are copious scenes of sex and nudity – none of which would be acceptable outside of subscription broadcasting in the US. Thematically the film changes too. It is not inconsistent, but has to tie up as many plot strands as possible (many of the incidental events are sidelined to concentrate on Betty and Rita). Lynch pulls a number of narrative tricks out of the hat that recall his conclusion to the European edit of the *Twin Peaks* pilot, the tying up of events in *Fire Walk With Me* and the twisted Möbius construct of *Lost Highway*.

Mulholland Dr. continues Lynch's love of mystery and secrets as well as the placing of young innocents in the role of detectives. This recognises the virtue in curiosity even if it leads to danger and law breaking. Betty and Rita are this film's counterpoints to Jeffrey and Sandy in *Blue Velvet* or Donna and James in *Twin Peaks*. They aim to uncover identities and discover the secrets in the lives of others. The twist on Betty and Rita's inquiry is that the identity they are investigating is Rita's, erased by amnesia following a terrible car crash. Like their counterparts the pair are not adverse to breaking and entering for the better good of solving the crime, but in all cases their actions have unforeseen and often terrifying consequences. In *Blue Velvet* Jeffrey is pulled into a dark world of sadism and crime, in *Twin Peaks* Dr Jacoby ends up being badly beaten and here the two girls come across a horribly decomposing body.

Mulholland Dr. does not treat time as linear but instead has its own internal logic that can be circular or malleable. By the time the film has come to a conclusion we know that the body Rita and Betty have discovered is actually that of Betty herself – although a Betty whose identity is now as Diane Selwyn. This duality in the identities of Betty/Diane and Rita/Camilla give the film its dreamlike logic – a logic that allows a person to discover another version of themselves decomposing in a bungalow. We accept that Betty and Diane are one and the same because our understanding of cinematic language sees narrative and temporal ties between scenes. When we see Naomi Watts fall asleep as Betty and cut to her waking as Diane our natural assumption is that this is the same person, that events are following in a linear fashion. Yet as we are aware, in *Mulholland Dr.* this is not necessarily the case. This could be a temporal jump and a change in character; so the film's internal logic is not breached but our understanding of film language and what we expect a filmmaker to depict is compromised. This is similar to the way that Annie can appear to Laura Palmer from the future without breaking the internal temporal structure of the *Twin Peaks* universe, for the laws of time in the Black Lodge are different from those of our world. In *INLAND EMPIRE* Nikki can catch the gaze of her prostitute doppelganger across a street, across time and across continents. *Lost Highway*'s Fred can ring his own doorbell while a version of him resides inside his house.

Some commentators have suggested that the whole of *Mulholland Dr.* is Betty's dream. So when does the dreaming begin? It could be argued that the entire film is a dream as indicated in the opening shots as the camera roams over red bed sheets before settling on a pillow, or that the whole construct is Diane's fragmented flashback at the moment she pulls the trigger. Or Betty could be dreaming at any point in the film between these events. Ultimately the question is academic and in many ways doesn't bear excessive scrutiny. Lynch is reliable as a director who tells us when something is a dream and when it is not. There is no doubt of Paul Atreides' visions or Dale Cooper's dreams. Similarly Laura's views of the Black Lodge and its denizens are clearly marked as 'real' because she is clearly not asleep. Perhaps then we should take *Mulholland Dr.* at face value because the indicators of a dream state are not obviously present. Instead we need to look at the way that Lynch shows us the perception of reality rather than reality itself – that in some sense we are waking dreamers. To this end *Mulholland Dr.* presents us with emotions in their bare state, manifesting feeling in its images. When the two girls huddle crying in the Silencio Club they are experiencing raw, unbridled, unexplained emotion. It is a feeling everyone may be familiar with and can relate to, but its random nature is unexpected in a neatly constructed cinematic environment. And given the choice between narrative cohesion and emotional cohesion, Lynch always plumps for the latter.

Films are by their very nature artificial and *Mulholland Dr.* acknowledges this by placing events in Hollywood, the 'Dream Factory'. Lynch has created a dreamlike vision which allows him the opportunity to comment on the Hollywood filmmaking process, its artificiality and its reliance on genre and cliché. Betty is an aspiring actress, Rita finds her name from a poster for *Gilda* and the entire film is based around the movie industry. Adam is a film director struggling with his need for artistic expression in the face of 'persuasion' from the criminal underworld. Coco is the decadent star of a bygone era living in an opulent world of stardom far removed from most actors' daily grind. This could all lead to another interpretation that the film's changes of character actually revolve around Betty's acting roles, and we know from her auditions that she is an accomplished actress. Having already critiqued the media in *On the Air* for comic effect, here the machinations of

Hollywood are shown to be no less absurd, but a lot less funny. Most elliptic of all is the Cowboy (played by Monty Montgomery) – again a twist on the farcical *Cowboy and the Frenchman* – a walking cliché made sinister because of his unclear intention and threats. He is menacing because a cowboy's presence in the context of a contemporary film is unexpected. His presence contradicts our understanding of genre, which states that a cowboy appears in Westerns, not a modern urban environment. In some respects he is analogous to the similarly anachronistic Mystery Man in *Lost Highway*. A link can also be seen between the characters of *Lost Highway*'s Mr Eddy, Mr Reindeer in *Wild at Heart* and the cold but deranged Mr Roque. Mr Roque is a malevolent movie mafia mogul with puppet-master control over the characters; like his counterparts he seems impervious to outside influence.

Lynch uses the film to deconstruct the incestuous 'Hollywood about Hollywood' films (aspiring star musicals of the 30s, *Sunset Boulevard* [1950], *The Player* [1992]) by embracing their premise but revealing the mendacity of Tinseltown navel gazing. To this end the only 'truth' comes from the Silencio Club – another in a long line of Lynchian stages. Theatre is often portrayed as truer than cinema but the Silencio Club suggests that even this is an artificial construct: the viewer is watching the performance and its audience through the medium of film, neither of which exist. The fact that we spend much of the time in the Silencio Club watching the two protagonists as audience members further reinforces the ideas of voyeurism that pepper Lynch's work. As a viewer the idea of watching the audience and not the film/play is counter to our expectations and further suggests the artificiality of this world.

Mulholland Dr. is not a film whose secrets are easily revealed, or even a film whose secrets can be revealed at all. Its internal consistency is at odds with our expectations of linear plotting in mainstream cinema and character identification. Its refusal to provide definitive answers makes it a natural successor to *Lost Highway*. Lynch likes to intrigue his audience with the same mysteries and secrets that intrigue his characters. Given that his conundrums are elliptical at best, the solution can depend as much on the viewer as the filmmaker. Lynch's job is to provide emotional truth and internal consistency; it's for the viewers to glean any solution from the information given.

WHERE IS IT THAT YOU THINK I WENT?

Rabbits (2002)

Directed by: David Lynch
Written by: David Lynch
Cast: Scott Coffey (Jack), Laura Elena Harring (Jane), Naomi Watts (Suzie)

In a static shot a girl rabbit, Suzie, quietly reads a book while her rabbit mother irons in the background. When her rabbit father comes in a slow interchange of phrases is passed between the three.

> 'The dark crawls. The socket drips. Disease. Hot. Electricity. Barbed. Wire. Sharp. Tearing open wet and wiggling. Dead dogs.'

Rabbits is an absurdist deconstruction of the sitcom – a nightmare reinterpretation of *Friends* or *I Love Lucy*. Traditionally the US sitcom 'filmed in front of a live audience' involves domestic situations and repetition of catch phrases filmed on two or three camera set-ups. It's a predominantly static medium. In *Rabbits* Lynch takes these limitations to extremes. The camera remains resolutely fixed throughout, creating a stage such as the studio audience attending a filming would see. In only one of the eight episodes there is a single insert shot to break the static tableau. Even though the films are clearly made without a live audience, Lynch mixes in the forced laughter, whoops and applause that are synonymous with the genre. Unaware as a viewer of the context of this particular sitcom, the audience interjection is disingenuous and unfathomable. They laugh uproariously at seemingly unfunny phrases and their group familiarity with the material alienates the viewer. They never seem even to talk with each other; each line is emotionless, uttered in isolation, so there is no interaction with what they are saying. The lines that are found to be amusing to the audience appear arbitrary. For example, in episode two a simple 'Oh?' from Jane provokes belly laughs, but 'It is still raining' does not.

Rabbits is full of the longeurs and pauses that punctuate cheaply filled television shows but once again these are taken to extremes. In episode one we watch Jane iron and Suzie read for two whole, unedited, minutes before Jack finally enters. In episode three over a minute passes before the lens focuses on Jack entering the empty room. Even then he takes an age to cross the floor and say anything. Partly this is to allow an uproarious response from the audience who whoop any time Jack enters – a Pavlovian response. This, then, is a comedy about comedy, one that criticises the bland sitcom by representing it at its most raw. It is so mannered and staged that the failings of the format are laid bare: the fact that other people dictate what you are to find funny, the artificiality of having an audience as part of the television space. This is even more farcical because the characters are all, as the title suggests, dressed in bipedal rabbit costumes, their ears casting huge shadows on the walls of their apartment. Neither do regular, less cuniculus sitcoms feature disembodied alien heads during blackouts, surreal songs accompanied by a giant burning match, silent phone calls or disingenuous dialogue.

Rabbits presents a different look at a familiar television staple, creating a world that is disjointed, strained and strange. An antidote to sitcoms, the world of *Rabbits* even found its way into *INLAND EMPIRE*.

Darkened Room (2002)

Directed by: David Lynch
Written by: David Lynch
Cast: Jordan Ladd (Girl #1), Cerina Vincent (Girl #2)

'My friend is crying. Do you see her?' our narrator asks directly to camera.

In a darkened room a girl huddles in the corner, mascara streaking down her face like a blackened mask. In front of her a doll lies spread-eagled, an umbilical cord trailing away, a dead, painted smile on its face. 'There's a hole in my slip and I haven't got any idea how it got there. Any clues?' Another girl enters the room and begins to castigate the crying girl. 'You do know that, don't you?' she constantly chides.

Darkened Room is one of Lynch's video experiments. The realisation that ideas can be sketched quickly and, most importantly, cheaply is one that appeals to him. Projects such as this can be made without studio interference and with complete authorial control – even the process of filming doesn't require a large crew. This, then, is democratic filmmaking from an artist freed of commercial constraints. *Darkened Room* was distributed on the Internet via www.davidlynch.com (a subscription site run by Lynch), and provides open access to the artist, albeit at a price. Video and the internet have given everyone the freedom to make and distribute films, but as a viewer how do you divide the wheat from the chaff? Just because more people can watch your work, it doesn't necessarily mean they will. There is also the problem of video quality. Considering Lynch's early films are so well shot it comes as a surprise to see video being used in such a way. But Lynch has a plan. Video is chaos. It contains random grain in the electric signals that makes for a textured viewing experience. This love of texture – we've seen it in much of his visual style – is taken to the medium itself. In *Darkened Room* the tension between video's audio and visual elements are more pronounced – the girl in the darkened room is accompanied by mood soundscapes but the narrator is filmed straight on with video quality sound that appears distractingly amateur, certainly jarring in a work from a filmmaker renowned for his exemplary use of sound.

INLAND EMPIRE (2006)

Having experimented with digital video as part of his Internet projects, Lynch decided to use the format for a feature length film. Ironically, while *Mulholland Dr.* started as a television production that was shot on 35mm film, this is a video (normally associated with television) production designed for cinemas.

Directed by: David Lynch
Written by: David Lynch
Produced by: David Lynch, Mary Sweeney
Edited by: David Lynch
Cinematography: Odd-Geir Sæther
Cast: Laura Dern (Nikki Grace/Susan Blue), Jeremy Irons (Kingsley Stewart), Justin Theroux (Devon Berk/Billy Side), Harry Dean Stanton (Freddie Howard), Peter J. Lucas (Piotrek Krol), Karolina Gruszka (Lost Girl), Grace Zabriskie (Visitor #1), Diane Ladd (Marilyn Levens)

'What the bloody hell is going on?'

In a dingy hotel in Poland a man pays for anonymous sex with a local prostitute. A young girl gazes, emotionally drained, at the flicker of a cheap television set playing sitcoms featuring bipedal rabbits. A world away, actress Nikki Grace is visited by her neighbour who tells her pointedly that she is to get the part of Susan Blue in a new film. Her insistent predictions prove to be correct. Working with actor Devon Berk and acclaimed director Kingsley Stewart, rehearsals and shooting begin on the film 'On High in Blue Tomorrows'. Devon, who has a reputation for romantic entanglements with his leading ladies, is warned not to become involved with Nikki: her husband is supremely jealous and potentially violent. It becomes apparent that the film, based on a Polish folk tale, is connected with a mystery. A different version of the production began some years earlier, only to be aborted by the sinister murder of the two lead actors. Nikki's attachment to the role creates rifts in her reality as her waking life and her narrative life begin to merge as filming progresses. Soon Nikki and Susan's psyches become intertwined. Against all advice, she begins a passionate affair with her leading man. Meanwhile other manifestations of Nikki and Susan are having problems of their own. A less affluent one finds herself pregnant, admitting her condition to her loathsome husband before seeking solace through phoning Billy Rabbit. Another self is eking out a dangerous life walking the streets in Poland, avoiding the casual, occasionally fatal, violence and the attentions of a ruthless cartel of people smugglers. All their paths undulate between separation and convergence as each of their lives tangentially alters the others.

It seemed like madness. David Lynch, renowned for his sumptuous, luscious visual detail, had turned to the dark side and embraced digital technology to make a feature film. Moreover this wasn't the multi-million-dollar studio set-up used by Lucas, Mann or Cameron but a modified Sony DSR-PD150, a very modestly priced camera by professional standards. Initially it seemed a backward step, one that would compromise the quality of the image. But for Lynch the advantages of digital production were manifold. After his experiments with the medium in *Darkened Room* and *Rabbits* he found the experience so liberating that elements of these shorts would filter into *INLAND EMPIRE*'s narrative as well as its visual style.

Digital has a relationship with electricity that is far more direct than celluloid, and the picture quality (which had improved considerably since the days of *The Amputee*) possesses a texture that combines chaos with electricity. In addition, his creativity would not be hampered by complex camera set-ups. While video doesn't obviate the need for quality lighting, technical knowledge and a large crew, it does streamline the process. Lynch could shoot 'on-the-fly', and did indeed undertake some of the camerawork himself. The cameras are lightweight, relatively easy to operate and the format cheap and reusable, so multiple takes and experimentation are easy to achieve. Editing can also be performed quickly.

Unlike many digital productions, INLAND EMPIRE was designed to be transferred to celluloid for projection, adding another layer of process to the image texture; the transfer also smoothes some of the jagged edges that plague low-resolution digital media.

'For me, there's no way back to film. I'm done with it,' Lynch says. 'I love abstraction. Film is a beautiful medium, but it's very slow and you don't get a chance to try a lot of different things. With DV, you get those chances. And in post-production, if you can think it, you can do it.'[17]

Lynch's move away from the medium of film is mirrored in INLAND EMPIRE itself. The film, in part, is about the shooting of a feature, 'On High in Blue Tomorrows', and charts the progress of its production, which is intertwined with the events that engulf the main character Nikki. We are, therefore, watching a film of a video watching the making of a film. The references to celluloid are very clear – the cameras are set up on cranes, the gate is checked at the end of each take and a room set aside to screen the rushes. Lynch plays with our notions of acting, the relationship between the viewer and the screen, and the nature of the film industry itself. At times the blur between acting and real life is presented as ambiguous or non-existent. Similarly to Naomi Watts in Mulholland Dr., Laura Dern portrays an actress who is very good at playing her roles. As a professional actress, of course, she should be, but as viewers, we are accustomed to a degree of theatricality signposting the 'acting' portrayed on screen. As we watch created roles, even the 'real' ones, any sense of objective reality is shattered because each reality becomes equally valid. Although each of these realities features different versions of Susan/Nikki they all intersect and become indistinguishable from one another, even as our understanding of which Susan/Nikki it is remains intact. The audience's hook into the Nikki/Susan we are watching lies in a combination of clothing, mannerisms, language and colour.

'That scene we did yesterday. It's happening tomorrow.'

This is a film about the act of viewing that takes *Lost Highway*'s themes into even deeper realms. When Nikki bursts into a cinema seeing rushes of the production, she sees the film we are watching, degraded and time-shifted a few seconds from her viewpoint. She is watching the film she is in and the events predict the next 'real' shots that we, the audience, will see. Lynch uses this motif several times throughout the film to nail specific instances in time, but this is the most audacious example. It makes the film's time structure, and even the film itself, seem familiar while the audience is watching it – like a recurring dream. The effect is haunting. In one scene the actress Nikki spies on herself from the opposite side of the street, herself as a prostitute caught up in a web of fear and intrigue. A link means that they catch each other's eye. Later the scene is played from the prostitute Nikki's story frame, seeing her more affluent self in the corner of her eye. That these events can't be simultaneous – they occur spatially and temporally at different locations and at different points in Nikki's story – is irrelevant. It could be that one of these is actually Nikki the actress playing Susan the character, but, even using that assumption, the situation is only internally consistent. But this is the nature of the puzzle that the viewer must unravel.

Like *Lost Highway* and *Mulholland Dr.*, *INLAND EMPIRE* is a time-distorted film about infidelity and psychosis. Through careful use of foreshadowing, Lynch creates a bizarre but believable dreamworld within which the audience and characters can lose themselves. In standard Hollywood films the technique of foreshadowing is used to create believability for a later scenario, or justify a character's ability. Lynch applies this premise to a variety of strange occurrences and objects that pepper his film. Were they simply to appear without precedence the results would lack internal plausibility and make the film feel weird for weird's sake. Instead, apparently disparate elements are imbued with a meaning – the watch, the cigarette burn, the 'Axx^{0}nn' logo. Lynch is fond of the process of discovering secrets and mysteries and viewers often imbue them with a significance that may or not be there – for example the defecating monkey from an earlier narration appears incidentally in the closing moments. It may be relevant or it may not; perhaps only time will tell.

Early in the narrative, the way that we can expect events to unfold in a consistent but fractured timeline is helpfully explained by Visitor #1 (Grace Zabriskie), allowing the apparent destruction of temporal verisimilitude to be absorbed by the audience and accepted as integral to the film's structure. When Visitor #1 imposes herself on Nikki she reveals that she is aware of how these time elements work, noting how Nikki will receive the part she wanted and that she will sit on the settee opposite, a day from now. When Nikki sees the next day, briefly, in a reverse shot, we know that time is not a linear concept in *INLAND EMPIRE*. It also implies that we should believe the other proclamations of the increasingly hysterical visitor – the house in the woods, the comment, 'Is it about marriage?' and the confirmation of a murder. Without the 'proof' that the visitor's earlier comments are correct the later comments would simply appear to be the ramblings of a mad woman.

From the outset *INLAND EMPIRE* marks a visual style that seems removed from Lynch's previous cinematic outings but much of it is derived from his less well-known projects. The opening black and white sequences of a prostitute and client feature faces that are blurred as though in motion or to hide the features – a technique that Lynch used to separate the image from the individual in his *Nudes and Smoke* series of photographs. Similarly his web experiments, *Rabbits* and especially *Darkened Room* – with its hand-held intimacy and oppressive questioning and framing, generating claustrophobic dread – have a direct relationship to the film. The former appears on the television channel at the film's opening and at many points within the film. Rather than just a passing reference, *Rabbits* is integrated into *INLAND EMPIRE*'s main text while also shedding some light on the web-based shorts. Initially the rabbits appear in their standard, single shot format but soon this space is breached and they are revealed to be as real as anything else in this world. At one point Nikki/Susan uses the phone only for it to be picked up by Jack Rabbit, which cues the audience's canned laughter. In the series we have never heard or known what is on the other end of the line and the audience laughter is apparently arbitrary and based upon repetition, but here it gains more apparent significance. Similarly the lit match burns its way through to the world of the rabbits, at least partially justifying its appearances in episodes five and seven of the series.

Rather like *Wild at Heart*, there are a series of small character stories that broaden the world and make us realise that events such as these could and do happen to others. From the outset the film is beset by stories and myths and these are centred, like *Twin Peaks*, on cabins deep in the woods and in alleyways beyond the safety of the main street. As with *Mulholland Dr.* there is a sense of doomed inevitability about a character's destiny, for not only are their fates predestined in some cases, but their demise has already happened, and their current state of life is a by-product of a non-linear time frame. Every tale told may thus be a reflection of a character's life or a cautionary tale to ignore at one's peril. 'On High in Blue Tomorrows' has, it turns out, been filmed before, in an ill-fated production called '4/7 (Vier Sieben)' based upon a gypsy folktale, where both the stars were murdered because of a terrible curse. Allegorical tales are told by Visitor #1, while Nikki/Susan's outpourings at the instigation of a grubby psychoanalyst in the A Room are marked by vignettes of explosive violence and sexual abuse. All add a menace of despair to the proceedings and flesh out the different versions of the characters.

A story of a mystery…
A mystery inside
Worlds within worlds…
Unfolding around
A woman… a woman
In love and in trouble

Part of the attraction in *INLAND EMPIRE* lies with the unravelling of the plot. This slow discovery may take several viewings – especially with a film so fluid in its application of temporality and cause-effect models. The sense of fear and wonder imposed on Lynch's 'innocent' characters (in the narrative sense) is reflected in the way that Lynch approached filming *INLAND EMPIRE*. None of the actors, including Laura Dern, were aware of the direction their role(s) were taking them from day-to-day.

'Each day was a different direction, each day was a different idea because we didn't have a script we were following. The truth is, I didn't know who I was playing — and I still don't know. I'm looking forward to seeing the film to learn more.'[18]

Every morning of filming Lynch would produce the pages necessary to get through that day's shoot, hence allowing the ideas to grow in an organic way. The flexibility of shooting on video meant that large sections could be completed in a single day rather than over several days, as is normal practice with film. Part of this is evident in some of the handheld scenes, which also provide a sense of claustrophobia – the very wide lenses that distort the backgrounds around the actors' faces almost imprison them in the camera. However *INLAND EMPIRE* was not a short shoot. The funding and the availability of the actors, coupled with the variety of location shoots in Poland, resulted in an unusually long production time. Having generated a great deal of footage, Lynch also spent a long time editing the film and overseeing its sound design. The sound design is typically engulfing and at times downright disturbing with its creaks, rumbles and drones – the crack of a light bulb in a roomful of prostitutes is horribly jarring. More surprisingly, *INLAND EMPIRE* is the first major Lynch production in nearly two decades not to feature an Angelo Badalamenti score, yet songs feature prominently on the soundtrack, breaking up the tension caused by long periods of atmospheric sound, notably when the prostitutes break into a rendition of *The Locomotion* before magically disappearing, or in the film's closing credits.

A daring and challenging work rich in texture and depth, *INLAND EMPIRE* proves that Lynch is not a director to rest on his laurels. The initial critical reception of the film when it premiered at the 2006 Venice Film Festival and Lynch received a lifetime achievement award was a combination of bemusement and contempt. But then *Wild at Heart* divided opinion when it received the *Palme d'Or* and both *Fire Walk With Me* and *Lost Highway* were treated with disdain on initial release. A David Lynch film is not a simple exercise in passive entertainment but an emotional and intellectual journey that requires an audience's serious attention and preferably multiple viewings, during which new meanings can be derived and additional emotions exposed. This is why, ultimately, Lynch's work has stood the test of time and will continue to do so, because it respects the intelligence of its audience and adheres to a very personal vision.

THE CLOUDS COME AND GO YET SOMETHING IS DIFFERENT

DAVID LYNCH PRODUCTIONS AND ACTING ROLES

Lynch has been involved in other film productions outside his own projects, as a producer, actor or both. Sometimes the credit is less for his role as a hands-on producer but more for his endorsement of the film or its filmmaker. In an increasingly homogenised world it is difficult to launch a career on the back of an esoteric that dares to be different. The David Lynch seal of approval can go some way to getting a film seen, no mean feat in an over-saturated marketplace. Take, for example, the independently produced documentary *I Don't Know Jack* (2002), a moving but candid tribute to the life and bizarre death, due in part to an altercation outside of a donut shop of all things, of Lynch luminary Jack Nance. Lynch appears in the film as an interviewee, recalling anecdotes about his ever popular star, but also above the credits is 'David Lynch Presents', a means of getting this labour of love seen by a larger audience.

Lynch's first production credit was on the short-lived but well recalled *American Chronicles* (1990), a Lynch/Frost documentary series showing the quirky but often gentle side of American life. It was with Frost that he would also put his name forward (as executive producer) for the slightly less wholesome *Hugh Hefner: Once Upon a Time* (1992), a portrait of the *Playboy* multi-millionaire's remarkable, and very American, life. Similar in many ways but more glitz-free is *Crumb* (1994), an honest and sometimes caustic look at the life of cult underground counter-culture comic artist Robert Crumb. At times very moving, this examination of the boundaries between art and acceptability really launched the career of director Terry Zwigoff, who later helmed the excellent and quirky *Ghost World* (2001) and the foul mouthed, but hugely enjoyable comedy *Bad Santa* (2004).

Lynch also served as executive producer on Michael Almereyda's vampire film *Nadja* (1994). This visually sumptuous black and white feature contrasts the political climate in (then) contemporary Romania with that of vampirism in New York. Almereyda's art-film background is on full display from his use of the Fisher Price pixel-vision camera (a children's toy sadly long out of production) to represent vampiric point of view shots, which contrasts with the brooding, crisp 35mm photography. Not only did Lynch executive produce this likeable blend of art and entertainment but also he appears briefly in the film as a security officer at a mortuary (a role he would reprise in a scene excised from *Lost Highway*), guarding the staked body of Count Voivoida Armenios Ceaucescu Dracula. It was not Lynch's first stab at acting. He had appeared in his own films as the doctor in *The Amputee*, a worried spice worker in *Dune* and, of course, as cryptic deaf Agent Gordon Cole in *Twin Peaks*, a role he clearly relished. Writer Harley Peyton recalls, 'At one point David wanted us to write a scene so that he could kiss Madchen Amick'.[19]

More importantly for his acting credentials he took a major supporting role alongside his then partner Isabella Rossellini in *Zelly and Me* (1988). The film is about a small, orphaned girl, Phoebe, growing up with her rich, fickle and occasionally cruel grandmother and her nanny Zelly (Isabella Rossellini). Zelly allows the girl to fuel her imagination by living out fantasies with her stuffed toys and giving her a passion for Joan of Arc, for whom the young girl feels an affinity. By night Zelly forms a relationship with Willie (David Lynch) who lives in the mansion close by. *Zelly and Me* is a charming, quirky fantasy that never becomes schmaltzy and doesn't provide a simplistic fairytale ending. Lynch's role as the boyfriend isn't stretching but he handles himself well, leaving the difficult roles for Rossellini and a great turn from young Alexandra Johnes. A fragile and delightful little film written and directed by Tina Rathborne, *Zelly and Me* received only limited distribution. As a result, however, she was one of the directors called up to work on *Twin Peaks*, directing two episodes for the series.

COMMERCIALS

Commercial production is a mutually lucrative business. Adverts offer the filmmaker an opportunity to work in a medium that is, by its nature, short and pithy but with budgets that can be immense. They offer the company commissioning the commercial the prestige of being associated with a known artist. Lynch's work in the field began in the late 1980s and has continued ever since. It's impossible to cover all of his work here but we can highlight some of the more unusual or interesting projects. The brief black and white campaign for Obsession For Men (1988) features readings of short passages from DH Lawrence, Ernest Hemingway and F Scott Fitzgerald on the nature of obsession, all set to a soothing orchestral score. Lynch became the perfume manufacturer's director of choice when he produced a jazzy extended advert for Giorgio Armani's Gio (1991), more conventional pieces for Yves Saint Laurent's Opium (1992) and Tresor (1993), as well as the bizarre pianist and panther promo for Jil Sander (1993) and the kitsch Pierre et Giles style short for Karl Lagerfeld's Sun, Moon and Stars (1994). In complete contrast the Georgia Coffee adverts (1991) tapped into *Twin Peaks* mania in Japan and featured a continuing story tracing the whereabouts of a missing girl. In only a few 30 second spots Lynch managed to create a new story, get in a deer head, introduce origami and save Asami from the Black Lodge, all while promoting canned coffee – 'brewed rich, tastes incredible!' The finale features Asami's escape and the rousing crowd pleaser 'Georgia all round'. Now that's celebrating.

Perhaps his darkest commission is the public information film made to keep New York tidy (1991), another black and white work which has all the brooding sinister atmosphere of *Eraserhead*. New York is filmed as a city from Hell because its inhabitants thoughtlessly discard litter. The results are legions of gnawing savage rats that breed below the surface. Totally without dialogue the short piece creates fear through its use of extreme close-up coupled with an ominous soundscape. A more pronounced contrast would be hard to find than in his 1993 campaign for Barilla Pasta featuring Gerard Depardieu serving instant pasta to a small girl who's fallen off her bike. Strangest of all, though, is an advert for Parisienne cigarettes (1998) featuring flames, hosing electricity, distorted speech, upwardly raining fish and a pair of strangely moving men in a brazen display of oddness that's part *Twin Peaks* at its nuttiest and part *Premonitions Following an Evil Deed*. Filmed using tactile old-fashioned effects techniques (mainly reverse film) it is a remarkable example of Surrealist film being used to sell cigarettes.

More recently Lynch has contributed to Nissan's 'Do you speak Micra?' campaign (2002) in a series of slick, blue neon adverts that blend words together to create new ones. It's the kind of word association so beloved of the early Surrealists. More extensive was a series of adverts, each depicting warped versions of reality, to launch Sony's Playstation 2 revolving around the cryptic tagline 'The Third Place'. It was a brave marketing manoeuvre from Sony (they hired a number of regarded film and video makers to launch the brand, including Chris Cunningham), particularly as Lynch wasn't renowned as a CGI director. The resulting films range from the quiet to the bombastic, in a variety of formats, both animated and live. The main Third Place advert is an odd journey, part *Eraserhead*, part Cooper's descent into the Black Lodge (there's even the thumbs up), culminating in a vomited severed arm and a talking duck man. Whatever the marketing, the adverts worked: Sony cleaned up the market for that particular generation of computer games consoles.

MUSIC VIDEOS AND PRODUCTION

It may seem unusual for a feature film director to make music videos – normally pop video directors yearn to be filmmakers – but the form offers the chance to free-associate and create non-narrative shorts. They also offer promotional opportunities. This certainly helped create the buzz surrounding *Wild at Heart* with Lynch's promo for Chris Isaak's *Wicked Game* intercutting shots of the singer with scenes from the film. Similarly the video for *Rammstein* features the group performing their song intercut with extensive clips of *Lost Highway*. The yellow blurs of the highway itself provide an extended introduction to the song, and more startling is the footage of the lead singer on stage and in flames, as disturbing as anything in the film itself. Whilst both these videos relate to Lynch's own films, he also produced an animated trailer for Michael Jackson's music video anthology *Dangerous*. The short clip features a tracking shot through a desolate red-swathed forest as a plume of flames spew forth the angel-winged head of Michael Jackson. He took a far more low-key approach when producing the video for Japanese singer Yoshiki's *Longing* and the single-take track of Massive Attack's *Unfinished Symphony*.

In addition to his video production for other musicians, Lynch has embarked on his own music production, which is unrelated to his film work. Also writing lyrics, most notable is his work with Angelo Badalamenti and Julee Cruise on the albums *Floating Into the Night* and *The Voice of Love* as well as a track for the soundtrack of Wim Wenders' science fiction road movie *Until The End of the World*. Other productions include a collaboration with sound engineer John Neff (*The Straight Story*, *Mulholland Dr.*) on an album of songs by Hildegard von Bingen with singer Jocelyn Montgomery and a rock/soundscape project *Blue Bob*, where the pair provide all the instrumentation and vocals.

THE ARTIST AND ANIMATOR

David Lynch began his career as an artist, developing his own style of painting, a sort of primitivist expressionist style. His experiments with art and form would fuel the desire to see his creations move following a chance breeze that seemed to animate the piece on which he was working – a black painting with green garden material emerging from the canvas. This revelation culminated in the experimental sculpture *Six Figures Getting Sick* and ultimately led to his career as a filmmaker, but he has continued to paint, draw, sculpt and produce artistic experiments through the years.

Many of Lynch's paintings are non-realist but he does add 'real' life to them in the form of natural textures (grass and grit), unusual man-made media (housepaint, sticking plaster, tar) and various insects. Like Dali he has an affinity with the insect world in his work. Early on in his career, he and Jack Fisk watched a moth trapped in a painting they were working on make little circles in an attempt to escape its sticky fate. Later works use actual insects in the painting; bees and flies form part of the canvases on show in his book *Images* (1994), and are even given individual names (in *Ricky Boards* and *The Bee Board*), whilst many of his paintings have insect connections (*Box of Bees, Antennae with Figure, A Bug Dreams of Heaven, Ant in My House* and so on). Linked with this is a fascination with decay and the grotesque, a common feature in his films but one given full rein in the realm of subconscious art like in the yawning, dripping, sexual wound of *Rat Meat Bird*.

Lynch's painted work is very tactile – textured and three-dimensional – but he has also continued with a number of experimental sculptures, some of which form the basis of his photographic work. Sculpture is a far more 'living' art than painting or film because it changes and reacts to its surroundings. In *Clay Head with Turkey, Cheese and Ants* a moulded head composed of mashed-up turkey and cheese is consumed over time by ants. The result is a slowly decaying sculpture and repro-duced as a series of photographs. *Man Thinking* comprises a toy with a bubblegum head. As Lynch says, 'There's something about chewed gum that's very organic looking – it's fleshy'.[20] In his most controversial sculpture, *Eat My Fear*, a white decapitated and mutilated cow has the words 'eat my fear' inscribed on its side. The piece, for the happily upbeat NYC Cow Parade, was deemed too upsetting and consequently banned, much to the consternation of the artist.

As with much of Lynch's film output his photographic work has a fascination with industry and industrial decay. Freed of the need for narrative, Lynch's photographs can show the beauty and horror in the abstraction of industrialisation. Even his nude work, a mainstay of the artist and art photographer (Philadelphia's own photographic genius Man Ray is principally remembered for his abstract nude photography), has a detachment that is rare in such art. In the *Nudes and Smoke* series the sexual nature of the model is masked by the veil of mystery, the industrial smog, the smoke that surrounds her. Like much of Lynch's work it is as enticing and seductive as it is disturbing and alien. The harsh colour entries in the series dissect identity away from the viewer, at once objectifying the model but denying a point of reference; the body becomes an abstract blur beneath a crisp, harsh surface.

Much of Lynch's work is concerned with wood, woods and secrets, so it's no surprise that this preoccupation has culminated in his production of wooden objects, particularly furniture, although the texture of wood also features in a number of his paintings. Some of Lynch's furniture design work can be seen in Fred's apartment in *Lost Highway* and also purchased, but be warned: the practicality of an unstable table may be less than its aesthetic worth.

Perhaps the most widely seen of his non-film projects, *The Angriest Dog in the World* is a masterpiece of minimalist cartoon writing. The four-panel comic strip ran in the *LA Reader* for nine years until 1992 (it now continues at www.davidlynch.com). The joy of *The Angriest Dog in the World* lay in the fact that the four panels remained essentially the same, week in and week out, with only the captions and speech bubbles altering. The first three frames feature the chained dog during the daytime, the final one at night. Each strip opened: 'The dog who is so angry he cannot move. He cannot eat. He cannot sleep. He can just barely growl… Bound so tightly with tension and anger he approaches the state of rigor mortis.' The 'plots' ranged from the whimsical to the disturbing, from the comic to the just plain unfathomable. The simple, black and white, harsh style of the strip, with its nervous, edgy lines and picket fence suburbia turned into a Dadaist battlefield, would later reflect the look of his animated series *Dumbland*.

Dumbland returns to the one-man animation studio feel of Lynch's early films *The Alphabet* and *The Grandmother,* but instead of using traditional stop-frame techniques Lynch employs Flash, the popular Internet content software. Flash's innovative way of re-using modular elements makes it an ideal choice for the home animator, simplifying the process of animation by allowing easy re-use and resizing of elements. That said, Lynch's approach to Flash was slightly more traditional and labour intensive, with each three-minute short taking days of work. *Dumbland* is as close to a one-man show as a world-renowned film-maker can get. It is also, as Lynch puts it, 'A crude, stupid, violent, absurd series'[21] – as is borne out by viewing any of the eight episodes. The hero of the piece is a vest-wearing, beer-swilling, aggressive, wife-beating thug who swears and intimidates his way through life. The language would make Frank Booth blanch. The overall effect is one of horrifying but humoured numbness.

A multimedia age should embrace multimedia artists. Although primarily known for his work in film and television Lynch has consistently cast his net further afield to embrace emerging technologies and revitalise old ones.

TRANSCENDENTAL MEDITATION AND WORLD PEACE

'There's an ocean of pure vibrant consciousness inside every one of us.'[22]

Perhaps it comes as a surprise to find that David Lynch, the creator of such graphic and controversial films as *Fire Walk With Me*, *Wild at Heart* and *Blue Velvet* should be concerned with world peace and the benefits of transcendental meditation. Initially the two ideas appear at odds but even a cursory examination shows that Lynch's films are concerned with heightened states of consciousness and redemption, of enlightenment and forgiveness. The world is a cruel place and Lynch reflects this, but there is always hope. The demise of many of Lynch's characters, including John Merrick and even Leland Palmer, culminate in their ascension to an all-encompassing light, an enlightenment that follows the hardship of their lives, as espoused in some Buddhist texts. In *Twin Peaks* Lynch gives Agent Dale Cooper an affinity with the Tibetan people and Albert Rosenfield a non-conventional roadmap of pacifism in the shadow of Gandhi. Alvin Straight's journey in *The Straight Story* is as much a pilgrimage taken in the long meditative expanse of the open road, the chudder-chudder of his lawnmower an industrial 'Om'.

'I have been "diving within" through the Transcendental Meditation technique for over 30 years. It has changed my life, my world.'[23]

Rather than merely indicate an affinity with the work of Maharishi Mahesh Yogi, Lynch has set up an organisation to promote his ideas. The David Lynch Foundation for Consciousness-Based Education and World Peace aims to improve the educational potential of children (and provide a respite for teachers) through TM, claiming better behaviour and academic standards, using simple silence techniques in a world cluttered with noise. Far more ambitious is the commitment and belief that TM can bring about the ultimate goal of world peace. Lynch also feels that TM helps in the creative process and has indicated that his twice-daily meditations have enabled him to be creative because they help remove fear and anxiety, enabling him to see a better, loving world.

'These negative things like anger and depression and sorrow, they are beautiful things in a story but they are like a poison to the filmmaker, they are a poison to the painter, they are a poison to creativity. They are like a vice grip.'[24]

Whatever the spiritual arguments for or against TM there is no denying that Lynch's adaptation of and belief in transcendental bliss have made an indelible mark on his filmmaking, both in terms of the process and the final result. Many filmmakers seek to change the world through their films and Lynch has gone one step further in his effort to achieve world peace. It has a price though: $7 billion to set up schools; still, a drop in the ocean compared to arms expenditure. As Lynch reasons:

'The formula for peace on earth is a group the size of the square root of 1 percent of the world's population. Since there are 6 billion people, you'd need a minimum of 8,000 peace-creating experts doing their job, uninterrupted. This group would be like a factory. It would produce peace on earth.'[25]

SHE'LL NEVER GO TO HOLLYWOOD – PROJECTS THAT WERE NEVER REALISED

Working in film and television is an expensive business, and investment in the wrong project can make or break a company. It should come as no surprise then that many more scripts are written and many more films optioned than actually get made. In some ways Lynch has addressed this issue by adopting a do-it-yourself approach to filmmaking with his website and *INLAND EMPIRE*, but over the years he has been involved with a number of projects that have either been put on hold or abandoned altogether. It's impossible to comment on them all, but we can present a selection of tempting 'what ifs'. How close these projects came to fruition varies enormously – at one point Lynch was asked if he wished to direct *Return of the Jedi* (1984) for George Lucas, a particularly exciting prospect for fans. Negotiations finished, however, pretty much as soon as they began when it became clear how limited his control over the project would be. He may have been afforded greater control on the planned *Dune* sequel, *Dune Messiah*, for which he was writing the screenplay, but it then became clear that the first film was not the anticipated success.

Another film that he never made was *Perdita Durango*, the sequel to *Wild at Heart*. Lynch had wanted to make the entire Sailor and Lula cycle but the chance passed and it was eventually shot by *Acción Mutante* (1993) director Álex de la Iglesia. Lynch's option on Barry Gifford's *Night People* may have led to their collaboration on *Lost Highway* but at one point filming the ambitious, multi-character open-ended novel was certainly considered. Another potential series came and went when he was offered *Red Dragon* but after pre-production work Lynch stepped away from the project, which went instead to Michael Mann, and was released as *Manhunter* (1986). Far more appropriate was Lynch's ongoing desire to film Kafka's classic *The Metamorphosis*, about a man who wakes up to find himself a giant bug. Although the material has been filmed before (as an animated film by Caroline Leaf and as a segment in Steven Soderbergh's *Kafka* [1991] among others), Lynch's take on the story would surely have been worth viewing.

Perhaps his longest unrealised project is *Ronnie Rocket*, conceived as a follow-up to *Eraserhead*, then *The Elephant Man*, *Dune* and *Blue Velvet*, continuing right up until *Fire Walk With Me*. It was never to be. Initially intended to star Dexter Fletcher after his turn as Bytes' boy in *The Elephant Man*, the role was eventually offered to Michael J Anderson, but the film was never made. It did mean, however, that Lynch found another actor to add to his entourage, and Anderson appeared in a number of later roles, most notably The Man from Another Place in *Twin Peaks*. *Ronnie Rocket* is almost a distillation of all of Lynch's themes, containing elements of electricity and mystery, of two worlds, separate yet connected, and including the most slapstick extremes of *On the Air* and *The Cowboy and the Frenchman*. A detective is searching for a way to the inner world, his qualification for entry the ability to stand on one leg, but his way is blocked by dubious companions, strange rooms, a train and, most frightening of all, the Donut Men, dealers of electric death. Meanwhile, diminutive Ronald d'Arte, a teenager with bad acne, is subjected to criminally poor plastic surgery resulting in lopsided ears and a shocking red mullet hairdo. To confound matters he needs to be plugged into the mains every 15 minutes and seems to have an affinity with electricity that can cause items to explode or produce beautiful music. He becomes Ronnie Rocket, an electric rockstar who befriends the tap dancing, glowing Electra-Cute. The combination of slapstick and violence, not to mention out-of-this-world weirdness (sinister knitters, the need to 'know the donut'), make for an intriguing prospect and there are so many breast fondlings, it could end up as a Russ Meyer film. Ronnie himself is not a traditional superhero despite his superhuman powers and an unusual outfit; he spends most of the film either blabbering incoherently or in a coma. His inactivity is apparently central to the plot but we'll never know for sure.

One of the more prolific partnerships Lynch has enjoyed is with Mark Frost. Aside from creating *Twin Peaks* and *On the Air* together, and producing the documentary series *American Chronicles*, they also collaborated on a number of unrealised projects. The first time Lynch met with Frost it was to discuss writing a screenplay about the cover-up behind the death of Marilyn Monroe and her relationship with the Kennedys based upon the book *Goddess: The Secret Lives of Marilyn Monroe* by Anthony Summers. The two set about fictionalising the text to make it more acceptable for studio backing, renaming the main protagonist Rosilyn Ramsey and retitling the piece *Venus Descending,* but to no avail. The thin veiling and the incendiary conclusion as to the identity of Monroe/Ramsey's killer gave the studios cold feet, though it's tempting to speculate that the dead body of a beautiful, wholesome girl full of secrets giving way to a larger mystery could have subliminally given birth to *Twin Peaks.*

Their next aborted collaboration, the all-out comedy *One Saliva Bubble*, reached pre-production but was never realised. Potential backers wanted *Twin Peaks* or *Blue Velvet*, and were not convinced that audiences would respond to the combination of ridiculous intellectual and puerile humour promised by the script. *One Saliva Bubble* concerns the consequences of a soldier blowing a raspberry at the climax of a scatological joke, one saliva bubble of which shorts some important equipment and sets a 24-hour countdown on a secret government satellite with potentially apocalyptic results. To avert the catastrophe we are introduced to a barking mad professor and his socks of many secrets, a group of Texans, Sammy 'The Stomp' (a blues musician) and a troupe of Chinese acrobats. Rival companies A and B are after the professor's ideas and the Heinz company are after a secret. The failure to shut the satellite down leads to the town being irradiated causing its denizens to swap identities but, crucially, no one apart from a pet dog can tell that this has occurred. Mistaken identity abounds. There are plenty of pie gags, a wind up pig/bomb, a plethora of 'Hugo first' jokes, an ice-rink that is in danger of digging to the centre of the earth and a tendency to rely on Heisenberg's Uncertainty Principle. Probably unmarketable, the failure of *On the Air* suggested that there was no audience for such outré comedy and the project was abandoned, as was a proposed television series *The Lemurians*, another comedy about a race of people so evil their land sank before Atlantis.

A further collaboration through the *Twin Peaks* connection came when Lynch worked with Robert Engels to produce the screenplay for *Dream of the Bovine*, a turn-of-the-twentieth-century, black and white film about three men who used to be cows. Described as bad, stupid and repulsing comedy no one seemed happy to back it, despite the low budget. Lynch would later be able to work on his own terms when tackling the one-man show *Dumbland*.

Perhaps one of the more intriguing unmade projects is *Woodcutters from Fiery Ships*, not a film or TV show but a computer game. As envisaged by producer Synergy, it was to be an immersive experience which would encourage the player to explore and even get themselves lost within the game. Part multimedia experience and part adventure game the player would have been drawn into the pipe-smoking world of the Woodcutters who are convinced you have witnessed bizarre events in a bungalow in Los Angeles. The game was deemed too 'boring' for the 'average gamer', however, a sad blight on an industry that once relied on innovation but increasingly falls back on generic convention, backed with multi-million-dollar budgets.

NIGHT THOUGHTS –
AN INTERVIEW WITH BARRY GIFFORD

There are currently three works by David Lynch that are connected with
your own and all of them came about in fundamentally different ways.
Wild at Heart was adapted from your book, *Hotel Room* was an original
teleplay and *Lost Highway* a collaboration. How do you feel these differences in approach affected the way your work was translated onto the
screen?

Well they're all very different. For *Wild at Heart* they bought the rights
to the novel. Originally Monty Montgomery, who became the producer
of the film, was intending to direct and showed it to David when they
were filming the pilot for *Twin Peaks* – it was called *Northwest Passage*
then. It's been reported in the past that David said, 'What if I like it?' and
Monty said, 'Well you can direct it'. So I think maybe it was a ploy to
intrigue David and hope that he would direct it. I talked right away with
David and he said, 'Well we've got to do this right now as we have a
window of time opening up'. Monty talked to me about perhaps collaborating on the screenplay so I said, 'I can't right now', as I was continuing to write the saga of Sailor and Lula, which as you know went on for
six novels. I was writing *Perdita Durango* which later became a film. So
David undertook to write it, which he did in six days. Then he sent me
the screenplay and basically it was very true to the book. The *Wizard of
Oz* stuff was integrated later and that was David's decision. The distrib-
utor Sam Goldwyn didn't want what they considered a true realistic or a
down ending, which is where Sailor and Lula split as they did right at the

---

end of *Wild at Heart*. The original screenplay was faithful to the book. One thing I did notice which was pretty funny when I showed up on the set on the first day he said, 'Well, Barry, how do you like the screenplay now?' And I said, 'I like it just fine but you missed out just one thing, the most important line in the story where Lula says "this whole world's really wild at heart and weird on top"'. He said, 'By golly, Barry, you're right!' In fact what David did was really brilliant. He inserted that line much later in the story, when Lula's alone in the Motel Iguana, Big Tuna, Texas, whereas I had it much earlier. Where he put it in was really appropriate for the film.

I hadn't seen the film, nobody had, until we were in Cannes. I had been in France, mostly promoting the novel, which was already a bestseller there. I'd been there three or four weeks doing a lot of publicity. I was shown the film along with three or four other people. I watched it at one o'clock in the morning in the Grand Palais where they were doing a test screening. David came up to me and said, 'Barry, I want you to tell me what you think of it with one word'. So the next day I said to David, 'Is it okay if I use two words?' And I said 'not boring'.

People forget at the time it was a groundbreaking film – it was the forerunner to any of Quentin Tarantino's work and many others. It really shocked people. It's hard for people to understand that now but I felt great about it. The film was the film and the book was the book. When people asked me what I felt David Lynch had done to the book I said he did nothing to the book. The book is still there. I think David really appreciated that attitude. It was the right attitude.

With *Hotel Room* that was a great opportunity too, because it was supposed to be this anthology television show. The mistake they admitted they made afterwards was that they didn't make three of my teleplays and have David direct all three of them. They stuck Jay McInerney's piece in there and I think Jay did a good job, but it didn't fit with the other two. The tone was not the same. In any case we did very well. When it was shown on HBO we were number one in our time slot and *Tricks* and *Blackout* were nominated for cable awards. David didn't change anything really. One little line in *Tricks* was added. He filmed them as I wrote them. I gave them three plays. The third one, *Mrs Kashfi,* based on a short story of mine, was not filmed. At first they were reluctant because it involved a child. It was a little problematic. I wrote *Blackout* in two days and it was only 17 pages long for a 30-minute show.

Normally screenplays run to a page per minute of screen time?
Normally, but by this time I knew how David's mind works and I knew it would stretch. It actually runs 45 minutes in David's version. It had to be cut down to 27 minutes for the purposes of the show, which ran at an hour and a half for the three. He took a 17-page script and it wound up 45 minutes. I really had the feeling about how David would approach it. I loved *Tricks* but I really felt with his filming of *Blackout* that I understood how he worked and how his mind worked. I began to study his paintings – that was all very important – and I understood that he was really a painter who wanted to see his paintings move.

Did that help when you were collaborating for *Lost Highway*?
Lost Highway made perfect sense because he hadn't made a movie in four years and he basically showed up at my door and said, 'Barry, let's write a movie'. He had some ideas and I had some ideas. He had held the rights to my novel *Night People* for over a year and he really wanted to film it. His daughter Jennifer had wanted to play one of the lesbians in the first part. I said, 'Why don't we just do something original? We're capable of that'. He agreed with me but he said he liked one of the lines in *Night People*, 'Lost Highway', which was not original anyway – it came from an old Hank Williams song – it was a sentence one of the girls in the novel speaks. And he liked that line at the end, which he put in the mouth of Mr Eddy: 'You and me Mister, we can really out ugly them sombitches, can't we?' That was all that was taken from the book. So we wrote it, we worked very intensely in Berkeley, mostly, in my studio. And, you know, I loved it. Every minute of it.

Novel writing is by its nature a solitary trade. How do you enjoy working with another person? Is it liberating or does it force you to curtail ideas you might be particularly fond of?

In fact it's particularly liberating. For me, I think it's great. After working for 25 to 30 years alone in a room, and writing all these books, it's sort of great making movies because you get out. Working with David was fun because we bounced ideas off one another. I've worked with other people subsequently and I like it. I like to play back and forth and often you inspire one another. Sometimes it doesn't work so easily or so well. There's usually one guy who sits at the typewriter and one guy who walks around the room. In the case of David and I we were both people who walked around the room, so sometimes we bumped into each other! But basically it worked really well, really easily. And then of course it's fun making the movie because you're out there with 100 people and it's like a little army and you're all going to war together. David's sets are particularly wonderful because it's like a big family. And we're all co-conspirators because we feel we're making something great, hopefully, and being part of cinema history.

He seems to work with the same group of people.

More or less. He works with people he trusts. And so it's always been nothing but a good experience as far as my dealings with David were concerned. We had a couple of other things that didn't fly, where they asked me to write something or rewrite something, but to tell the truth, I have nothing controversial to say about working with David. It's always been a pleasure. We each respect the other's work and each other. In fact, when we were putting together *Lost Highway*, I remember my son had his 21st birthday party at Dave's house. It all went very well.

We understand both David Lynch and yourself had ideas for *Lost Highway* before you met, but that neither of you liked the other's! Is that story true and can you recall any of these?

No, what happened was, and David has spoken about this, after we wrote the first draft we each looked at it and realised there were things we didn't like about it. We had a break because I had to go to Spain to do promotion for a novel, and then I came back and we'd had a chance to each look at it, to reappraise our approach to it. Then when we got back together we kept the things we most valued. And we were in virtually complete agreement about it. This is my memory about it. In other words, what should go and what should stay, the direction in which it should move and the fact that it had to be very straight. It had to be played completely straight without any hokum or comedy intentionally written. That's how it was done.

When did the idea to make the Möbius strip narrative in *Lost Highway* come about?

Well that just naturally, organically came about. I don't remember saying, 'Oh that's just like a Möbius, let's do this as a Möbius strip is constructed'. Later, when we saw what we had, we could see the similarity.

Every time you view *Lost Highway* you get more from it. It's incredibly rich and textured.

That's also the intention. A lot of people found it difficult or teasing in a way – that we were playing with people. I was sort of surprised by a lot of very smart people who reacted adversely to that picture. They thought we were messing with them in some way or trying to play some trick on them. But no, it was very straight, very straightforward. In fact people like Zizek wrote a book about it and there are courses in universities taught just on *Lost Highway*. In fact one of my sons was in one at UC San Diego. Later his professor found out who he was – he got an A in the class, by the way – and one of his friends told the professor, who was French and had written some big long article on the film. He gave it to my son who passed it on to me and wanted to talk to me and answer all these questions about the film. Of course I refused.

In *Wild at Heart* much of the incidental detail, the kind that usually gets thrown out of conventional Hollywood adaptations, remains. It's a delicate balancing act to relate all the characters but still maintain the attention of an audience – but it really works in this film, where everyone is interconnected and all the pieces of the story fit.

Of course *Wild at Heart* held together because it was a novel, you had the construction already. The structure was already there and nothing was random. So David had that to work with. To go back a step further, even when he decided to change the ending and make it a happy ending, he called me and said, 'Well, do Sailor and Lula get back together ever?' and I said, 'Yes, of course they do. In fact I'm writing them going into their 60s – the whole saga is like one big novel'. So he said 'great'. Not that he needed justification, but it really helped in that sense, when he wrapped on the happy ending where they come back together. My ending is in the movie.

The dialogue is identical.
Right. And then there's that coda when Sailor comes back. Then working on *Perdita Durango* was entirely different. You know David had said to me during the filming of *Wild at Heart*, 'Well, let's go on and do *Perdita Durango*, we'll do everything'. But we didn't. *Perdita Durango* was a bestseller in Spain and bought by the biggest film company at the time in Spain. The director originally assigned to the project was Bigas Luna. Bigas and I became great friends and we hung out together a lot in Spain. And Javier Bardem, who was then the star of Bigas' movies, was a young actor in many of his films and the original choice to play Romeo Dolorosa. So I got to know Javier and we became great buddies and we spent a lot of time together. He really was that character of Romeo. As it turned out he and the producer had a dispute and Bigas was taken off the project so it lay there for a couple of years. Then it was offered to Pedro Almodovar who is a good friend of mine. But the producer Andrés Vicente Gómez did not want to sell it to Almodovar. He wanted to retain control. So then he gave it to Álex de la Iglesia, a hot

young director who was 29 years old. And the movie was okay. It is what it is. With *Perdita Durango* I think there's some wonderful things in there and some really inspired things but it's not the movie I would have made. And while I respect Álex de la Iglesia I believe that it was a great movie for Javier Bardem. I think it was a brilliant, brilliant performance by Javier. And that made him a star in Spain.

It had quite a lot of trouble with the censor here in Britain.
As far as that film's concerned there's some great stuff in it. I've only seen it in the uncut version of course. Let's go back one step to *Wild at Heart* – don't forget that scene when Johnnie Farragut is killed was much, much longer. It went on for three minutes, the torture at the hands of Juana. That was pretty ghastly and grisly and went on for a very long time and wound up getting cut down to 30 seconds.

Even those 30 seconds are very powerful.
It's still very powerful and I think it works just as it is. Apparently at a test screening people went running out of the theatre during that scene. Monty and the other producers had even said to David in advance that they were afraid of the scene and David realised after that that he wasn't going to be able to keep the audience in their seats because it was too gruesome. And so he cut it down to 30 seconds and it works just as well. With *Wild at Heart* David filmed every scene in the book. I never saw a lot of it but he said they filmed everything and then it was four hours long, so they had to cut it down.

Now I'm talking with Guillermo Arriaga, who wrote *Amores Perros*, *Babel* and *21 Grams,* about him doing *The Sinaloa Story*. The thing is, it's a Mexican story. Those are very hard books, very difficult, very tough. I don't think the climate is really right for it these days.

Sailor and Lula are terrific characters – they feel so wild and passionate. When you were creating them where did they come from? Do you empathise with them?

Well, the true story – it's been reported differently at different times – is that I was in North Carolina on the Cape Fear River staying in a little hotel. I was down there doing a work of journalism, writing a piece about deep-sea fishing tournaments. And I woke up one morning and heard a conversation going on. It was erroneously reported that I heard conversation from another room, but that's not true. It was entirely in my head. It was these characters Sailor and Lula speaking to one another. It was just like they were in the hotel room, the Cape Fear hotel. And I sat down and started writing down that conversation and that's how it was born. And I never did write the book on deep-sea fishing. I'm sure they were based, in part, on people I've known or information that just crystallised at this propitious moment and there they were. So I had to remain true to them and that's what I did. And it went on for 600 pages. I never thought I'd ever really go back to it. They make a brief kind of cameo in my novel *Baby Cat Face*, a prequel to *Wild at Heart* actually, while Lula's still in high school. But right now I'm writing what will be the seventh Sailor and Lula novel. It's Lula at the age of 80, she's reflecting on her life and she has a new adventure with her old friend Beany who appeared in the beginning of *Wild at Heart* and in *Sailor's Holiday*. So she's still with me. She's the enduring one. Lula's my favourite character of any I've created in the sense that she seems the truest, the one for whom I have the greatest affection and I'm glad she came back.

She comes across as the most honest character. Rather than ciphers, your characters come across as very genuine.
Well, thank you. I mean Lula would force Sailor to be honest about himself and about things. I think that's something that Lynch brought out correctly in the film version. That Lula's really the strong character. She's a survivor after all.

Your novels are full of rounded characters sketched in a succinct manner; there seems to be a democratisation of characters that is

humane and shows how we are all in some way connected. Film usually tends to focus on a few individuals. How do you reconcile this when writing a screenplay?

The writing of screenplays and the writing of fiction have very little in common, only the fact that they both necessitate the use of words. It's an entirely different language and you know the simplest way to say it is that you're going to see the movie and you're going to be reading the book. If you read fiction you have to use your imagination in order to visualise the characters, how they must look. Maybe they are described, maybe not, but you have to imagine what their voices sound like, you have to bring something to the party. With a movie, basically you can just sit there and let the images wash over you. I think this is a good moment for me to reiterate what I said before in that one reason I think David and I got along so well is that we both share the idea of the experience of surrendering yourself to a film. You enter this kind of dream chamber, you just let the images wash over you and you have to surrender entirely to it. It's like a dream and you enter into a dream world or a trancelike state. Now if it's a bad dream you can get up and walk out – you are not trapped like you are in sleep – but this is definitely the idea that I always carry with me about film. So when Lynch said a similar thing I knew I had found the right person to collaborate with at that moment.

People have asked me to write for film because they think the dialogue is true – they like the dialogue. But it was funny because one time Matt Dillon and I were at the Toronto Film Festival with *City of Ghosts* – the film that he directed and I co-wrote – and when someone asked a question Matt made this remark that 'Barry's so good at structure', which I really don't think about. In other words the structure comes about spontaneously. I don't think you have to have the first sex scene by page 30 if you're writing a novel, or the first sex scene in the first 13 minutes of the film, or after page 80 in the screenplay you have to go to act three. I'm not a formulaic writer, as you know, so I let the characters dictate the action and what seems natural to them. As the characters that I've created, I try to remain faithful to them. Recently somebody was saying to me, 'how does this book end – the one you are writing now with Lula?' and I said, 'Oh, gee, I don't know'. They said, 'Don't you know where you are going with this book?' and I said, 'Absolutely not. I know she's going from North Carolina to New Orleans but I'm not sure what happens along the way and I'm not sure what's going to happen when she gets there'. I like it to remain a mystery. I like to be surprised. I like to find out what happens, just like anybody else. At the risk of sounding disingenuous as I say this, I'm telling you the truth, I really don't know where it's going. I might make notes in the margin whenever I'm writing a screenplay or writing a novel and think about scenes that I'd like to write or places I'd like to go or things I'd like the characters to say if the moment comes, but I've got loads of this stuff that I never use.

It must make the writing process very enjoyable as well.
Well, for me it'd better be enjoyable! I've been writing since I was 11 years old. I know there are some people who hate to write – some great writers who hate to write. It's real anguish for them. Well, it can be anguish for me too, at different times, due to different situations. I'm not saying that it's easy at all. In fact what I've always done is sneak up on it. I don't know how else to say it. I sort of sneak up on myself and then somehow it gets done. And I like to leave it a little to the unknown, a bit of a magical process. I know there are people who write books about how to write *ad nauseam* and what writing means to them and they love to talk about it. I hate it. You know I'm not very analytical. I'm not an academic. I don't have a college degree. I didn't learn how to write in any workshop or at any university. I just started writing these stories when I was 11 and I'm still doing it. I don't hang around with writers either. The thing is, I'm not necessarily Mr Natural – it's just I have a vivid imagination and I have a certain history which lends itself to being able to create these stories and these characters. So that's how it came about. There are no rules here. It doesn't matter. You can go to 50 universities, I have

nothing against that. I think it's great, it's wonderful. You can be a shoe salesman and write a great novel or film, or become a director. However it happens, it happens, who cares? It's open to anyone. Anybody can try it. As long as you do well by yourself and others then you've been successful. There aren't any rules, there shouldn't be.

David Lynch's films are among the most perfectly sound-designed films, *Lost Highway* in particular. In the screenplay the soundtrack is sometimes referred to directly (for example using Lou Reed's *This Magic Moment*). How much did you discuss sound when writing the screenplay? Does sound enter into a written medium?
We did discuss sound and especially music. And I played a lot of music for David. *This Magic Moment* was written by Doc Pomus. I was playing it at the time and gave David a CD. Or he got it after hearing my anthology of songs written by Doc Pomus by different performers. That happened to be on it and it was perfect for that situation. It was the same thing for *Wild at Heart*. The music supervisor came to my house and I played many, many records for him of singles and albums and stuff like that. He made a list of it all. I began as a musician and so I'm very close to the music. If you look at *Wild at Heart* there's all kinds of music referred to.

The music both enters the diegesis and complements it too.
It's through all my books continually. I think David liked that and he's similar in that regard as far as sound is concerned. A friend of mine was just at the Venice Film Festival where David showed *INLAND EMPIRE*, and there was an interview with him where he was talking about the movie and that the sound was integral to the film, how important sound is. He was always very strong minded about this, he worked closely with Randy Thom, one of the great sound designers, on *Wild at Heart* and this was always a principle of filmmaking with David and with some others too.
Here's a funny little anecdote. *Lost Highway* was playing in a little

cinema after the first run in Paris and a friend of mine had not seen the film. I was living in Paris at the time. It was unfortunate having to see it in a cinema on such a small screen but it was the only place it was playing at the time. We went in and it was a pretty bad print. It had been used a lot. So it began and the sound was really too low. I went back to see the manager or someone in the theatre and I said, 'The film has to be louder'. So they made it a little louder. And I said, 'It's got to be louder, this isn't going to work'. I went back again up to the projector booth and I said, 'Listen, you've got to make this film louder, it's really got to be loud'. And the guy was exasperated and turned to me and said, 'Who are you to be saying this?' I told him I wrote the film. He said 'oh' and then they cranked it up. It was really funny and the reason it couldn't be too loud was because it was next to a restaurant and apartment house and they would get complaints. David wants it to be loud. It makes a big impression on the audience. It's like thunder. You hear this bang, bang, bang and those quick sounds that you get in *Lost Highway* and *Wild at Heart* specifically. It really unnerves you and can shock you – it's terrific.

It's the contrast that has an impact as well. There are moments of quiet and very loud moments as well, and very intense music.
Look at the scene in *Lost Highway*. I remember Mary Sweeney, sitting with her in the editing room on *Lost Highway*, and David had wanted to cut out the scene from when Pete Dayton was brought back from jail and he's sitting in his backyard. He's just sitting in the backyard of this little house and watching the little ducks in the swimming pool and the Brazilian music is playing and it's just very sweet and wistful and there's no dialogue at all. It's such a beautiful little scene and Mary said to me, 'You know, isn't this the perfect David Lynch moment?' She was right and I said it was really beautiful and I said it's got to remain in the film. It's a very quiet lovely thing with just this scarred character sitting there.

It's a pivotal scene in the movie. It's at the point of the change and a lull after all the excitement as well. You've got all the intensity of the previous scene and then the audience have time to compose themselves.

Exactly. Because it's the transitional moment. The seminal transitional moment and the fact that it's done without bombast after all of that horrible transmogrification that we see in the jail cell. Then it becomes serene and quiet and now we're able to make the transition. It's like walking across a little bridge.

Do you write to music?

Often, often. Not with lyrics usually. It depends on my mood. If something's working I'll stick with it for days at a time.

THERE'S ALWAYS MUSIC IN THE AIR – DAVID LYNCH AND SOUND IN THE CINEMA

The richness of film lies in the way it draws on all elements of the arts to provide an intoxicating melange of sight and sound, enticing the viewer with a cavalcade of delights. It is the combination of visual and audio that delivers the message of a film. Much film analysis centres on the image, the acting or the narrative, aspects that are comfortably discussed in relation to the fine arts, theatre or literature. Discussions about sound tend to focus on the score as if it's apparently analogous to music in isolation. It is not. Sound in the cinema is often ignored and most people fail to realise its importance.

The use of sound in film can be roughly split into a number of elements. Most obvious in narrative cinema is that of dialogue, which can be internalised as well as on-screen. This can be more than the simple rendering of a script – the backwards-running dialogue of *Wild at Heart* or *Twin Peaks,* for example, or the indecipherable vowel mispronunciation of Gochktch in *On the Air.* Then there's diegetic sound, where the sound is part of the narrative itself. This is either naturally occurring relational sound or even music as it is performed, as with the band in *Wild at Heart.* Non-diegetic sound has no obvious relation to what is occurring directly on screen – the soundtrack creates the mood and feeling of the film or incidental noises are designed to have an emotional effect rather than a relational one.

Finally there are sound effects and foley (synchronised sound effects). It's impossible to overemphasise the importance of David

Lynch's contribution to sound design within cinema. As a director who moved into filmmaking from visual arts, it might seem unusual that he would pay such close attention to sound and innovate to the extent that he has, but it is integral to creating his cohesive cinematic world. Lynch soon realised that the medium of film could offer many more creative possibilities than the purely visual. From the simple repeating siren of *Six Figures Getting Sick* to the complex concert of *Mulholland Dr.*'s Silencio Club, the combination of scoring, sound effects and songs integrate to create soundscapes that are a fundamental part of each of Lynch's films.

The diegetic sound that emphasises the nature of staging, theatre, artificiality and voyeurism in Lynch's work is further enhanced by his use of music as part of the story. It's interesting that Lynch will often allow this diegetic use of music to be complemented elsewhere by reprises that are non-diegetic in nature, as though they are memories of the music, recalling themes and motifs. In *Blue Velvet* Isabella Rossellini sings the film's titular song on stage, diegetically, in front of an audience that includes Frank, Jeffrey and, ultimately, us. Its presence is felt non-diegetically throughout the film, recurring as an orchestral leitmotif and providing the soundtrack to the opening credits. Direct use of songs extends further into *Blue Velvet*'s story. Frank Booth threatens Jeffrey to the lyrics of *In Dreams* as it plays on the car stereo, a song that has previously been mimed by Ben. It turns an apparently sweet song into something entirely more sinister as he spits out the lyrics, his face scrawled with lipstick smudges. These two old songs provide much of the backdrop for the characters' motivations in the film, particularly Frank, and also Dorothy, who literally does see blue velvet through her tears. *INLAND EMPIRE*'s song and dance prostitutes pre-empt their act by using song lyrics in casual dialogue – 'You've got to swing your hips now'. Similar sound themes occur in *Wild at Heart*'s appropriation of Elvis songs, culminating in Sailor's rendition of *Love Me Tender* as he finally commits to a life with Lula.

In many films it is the non-diegetic sound that creates the mood for the piece by triggering audiences' responses to certain sounds. Lynch is not alone in adopting this practice but he also uses diegetic sound to create an atmosphere – it is the combination of the two that makes some scenes unbearably powerful. Maddy's death in *Twin Peaks* is accompanied by the cold ominous click of the record player, warning the audience of the evil that is coming. This contrasts with Julee Cruise's ethereal singing at the Roadhouse, which tells both us and the Twin Peaks' residents that something tragic is happening. The combination of these two diegetic soundtracks is charged with emotion and relates the events temporally. Underlying them, though, is a subtle drone that acts as a non-diegetic trigger for an audience response. When Sarah Palmer is drugged and Laura raped in *Fire Walk With Me*, the regular beat of the swirling fan provides a diegetic pulse that accompanies the entire scene even as the moody non-diegetic bass notes help reinforce unease in the viewer.

Non-diegetic music is also crucial to defining a film's style. Lynch often uses pre-composed songs in conjunction with a scored soundtrack, a practice that is common but relatively modern in cinematic terms. What makes his use of non-diegetic music so interesting is the juxtaposition of different styles from different times, an ear for the right song matched only by Martin Scorsese, Wes Anderson or the postmodern referencing of Quentin Tarantino. In *Wild at Heart* the score is varied, representational and constantly a fundamental part of the film. It opens with sweeping strings to give a sense of majesty, and almost romance as seductive flames tumble on the screen, before it segues into *In The Mood* at the party. The music becomes increasingly integrated into the soundtrack, mirroring the characters and their actions. This contrasts with Angelo Badalamenti's dark, touching and elemental classical compositions, what we might term a 'traditional' score, and Chris Isaak's contemporary but retro-sounding tunes, further recalling the Roy Orbison songs of *Blue Velvet*. Indeed Badalamenti has been vital in realising the original parts of the scores from virtually all the films post-*Blue Velvet*, as well as the television work, making him as important a collaborator in Lynch's work as, say, Danny Elfman in Tim Burton's or Nino Rota in Fellini's.

Lost Highway in particular uses popular and contemporary music to reinforce the characters' feelings. Indeed the soundtrack for the film remains to this day one of the most astonishing and varied committed to celluloid. When Pete recalls catching sight of Alice, the film glides into fantasy slow motion as Lou Reed's version of *This Magic Moment* plays, emphasising his feelings and emotions. Similarly Marilyn Manson's pounding, relentless and sleazy cover version of *I Put a Spell on You* accompanies Alice stripping for Mr Eddy, adding to the already dank sordid air of coercion. Lynch uses aural motifs that often enter the diegesis. This Mortal Coil's wonderfully evocative *Song to the Siren* is used extensively as a fleeting motif through the entire running time before being employed extensively at the climax. The song's lyric 'Here I am...' is repeated as a refrain, extended notes rising and falling ethereally. As Alice rejects Pete he chases after her only to encounter the Mystery Man in the cabin. 'Here I am,' he announces in a flat deadpan tone, an example where the soundtrack has directly invaded the film's world. In contrast to the use of music in *Lost Highway, Dune* is perhaps the one film where the music doesn't work – Toto's loud, pompous and bombastic score overwhelms the film rather than complements it.

Foley effects and sound design are always critical to the understanding of a film and the filmmaking process, but are often only taken in subconsciously by the audience – usually their very purpose is to be transparent. The viewer tends to only notice the absence of foley, or deliberately inappropriate use (e.g. a shooting gun sounding like a duck in a comedy draws attention to itself because of its illogical lack of verisimilitude) but it can have a profound effect on the tone of the film. It's often the sound that enhances the viewer's imagination and can give them a false impression of what has actually been seen on screen. For example, the sound of the impact of someone being hit gives an indication of how severe it is. Hence the squelch sound of Andy's head as it is lodged into the coffee table in *Lost Highway* adds to the sheer awfulness of his death as much as, if not more than, the visual impact. Lynch also likes to make use of the representation of sound, in some way a deliberate use of false sounding foley. In many of his films screams don't sound like they do in real life – they are accentuated representations of screams or distorted versions of them. Similarly Lynch uses sound metaphors, particularly animal or industrial noises, to create a greater impact than realistic sound effects. The stampede that opens *The Elephant Man* mutates the bellowing calls of the elephants and replaces their relentless charge with the sound of machinery pounding. In *The Grandmother* the parents can only articulate through animalistic barks and shouting. Killer Bob in *Twin Peaks* is represented by animal sounds – when he attacks his victim it's with the slow roar of a wild beast.

As Lynch alters the pace of the visual elements of his films, he also alters the sound accordingly. Slow motion, for example, is often accompanied by slowed sound. It seems the obvious thing to do but is surprisingly rare in film. Lynch also employs the equivalent of a sound close-up. In *Wild at Heart,* as Sailor or Lula drag on a cigarette, the images show close-ups of a match sparking fire and burning tobacco, accompanied with a rushing, crackling sound as loud as gun-shot and a bush fire. Similarly the rhythm of the sound matches the pacing of the visuals and editing. As Sailor and Lula speed down the highway, the lines on the road zooming by, alternating between dotted and solid stripes of paint, the visuals precisely match the rat-a-tat stutter of the heavy music.

Ubiquitous throughout Lynch's oeuvre is the use of rumbles, hums and bass-tones, of industrial clatter and the sound of electricity arcing. Sometimes these effects relate directly to what the viewer sees – the factories of *The Elephant Man*, the spark of electricity or the strobing of a flickering light bulb in *Eraserhead* or *Mulholland Dr.*, the fizz of a neon sign in *Twin Peaks*. More often these sounds come from direct physical association to the viewer. They are there to create an uneasy tension, to make events seem ominous or on the brink of chaos. They underline the mood of a film and harbour impressions of impending and pervasive catastrophe. These sounds are designed to enhance the mystery, to put the viewer on edge. Some of the sub-bass work in *Lost Highway*, *Eraserhead* and even *Dune* has the effect of physically vibrating the viewer's diaphragm should the sound levels be at the volume intended, i.e. very loud. These sounds then are emotive responders for the audience – even as they are causing an emotional response they are nonetheless re-emphasising the manipulative nature of film. A more transparent use of sound than this comes about through Lynch's love of staging, as it emphasises the artificial nature of the medium. This is not just in the visual sense but in the aural one too. The scene in *Mulholland Dr.*'s Silencio Club is the musical equivalent of Magritte's painting *Ceci n'est pas un pipe* as Rebekah del Rio apparently sings a Spanish version of *Crying*. When she collapses on stage, unconscious, the singing continues. This is not a live performance. As the compère says, 'It is an illusion', even as his off-screen orchestra play in time with his gestures. In *Rabbits* the unseen audience reaction to the staged sitcom is clearly just as artificial.

Cinema is the blend of sound and vision. Although sound is often overlooked in favour of its flashier visual counterpart it is as relevant to the meaning and effect of a film as the picture. David Lynch's exemplary use of soundtrack and sound design makes him one of the most innovative proponents of the form working today.

PRETTY AS A PICTURE –
DAVID LYNCH'S VISUAL STYLE

Film is often marketed through images. Even though it also relies upon aural elements, it's the look of a film that usually entices an audience, promoted through visual media such as books, film posters, magazines and the Internet. It is the visual style of a film that often attracts the most analysis so in many ways the look of a film can be crucial to its reception and success. David Lynch began his career as a fine artist and his films have always had a strong sense of visual style, even within the conventions of narrative cinema, which tends to foreground effects work or script-based character development over aesthetic verisimilitude. His early films highlight these artistic roots. *Six Figures Getting Sick* in particular is more of an art installation than a film: animation combines with live action to construct an overall story that is more concerned with artistic than narrative coherence.

Lynch has always mixed his media, either in his painting or in his filmmaking, to achieve the results that he desires visually. While *The Elephant Man*, *Dune* and *The Straight Story* are exquisitely filmed using conventional film stock, Lynch has explored the use of video to create textures for *Fire Walk With Me* and *Lost Highway*. He has now progressed into and is embracing the digital age, working with digital video (DV) and loving the freedom it affords him. It's a natural progression – the move from filming actual textures to using the media itself as the texture. Electricity has always been a chaotic element in his films both aurally and visually, and the harsh chaos produced on video's electrically produced images contrasts with the organic grain of traditional film stock. Video feels more industrial than film, but it is also more accessible and allows for greater spontaneity and improvisation. He usually works with the most accessible media; in his early career this was film, now it is, without doubt, DV.

Complementing the medium, Lynch employs physical textures to enhance the visual style. *Blue Velvet* opens with the literal texture of crushed rippling blue velvet and *Fire Walk With Me* with the blue 'white noise' of a television screen. He is particularly keen on depicting objects that are not perfect. Chaos has a beauty that's at once fascinating and dangerous. *Eraserhead* and *The Grandmother* are full of shots of such unusual images as well as the adoption of natural textures in unnatural environments, for example, little piles of earth located indoors. These provide a harsh organic feel to the film's visual space. Another way of achieving these organic textures is through the use of extreme close-ups, most apparent in *Wild at Heart* as a burning match ignites Lula's cigarette and then the paper and tobacco burn the screen like a flaming sun. In *Twin Peaks*, many of the guest directors took cues from Lynch's visual style and several episodes open with an extreme close-up of an everyday object, a ceiling tile for example, and pull back slowly to reveal the item. It provides the audience with an unusual perspective on something ordinary as well as a mini visual mystery. Another texture that has become apparent in Lynch's more recent work is achieved through the use of superimposition. The very start of *Mulholland Dr.* shows a group of youngsters jiving together, layers of images superimposed over one another to almost kaleidoscopic effect.

Use of colour is always important, providing visual schemes for the viewer to relate to certain events and characters. *The Grandmother* used colour stock but it appeared to be filmed in black and white, allowing the splashes of colour to have far more impact. The white make-up of the main characters emphasises their red lips and the rims of their eyes. Lynch contrasts this with extreme use of very strong colours – the orange of the boy's soiled bed, the sun and the watering can. Most of

Lynch's films have colour themes and primary colours often dominate – in *Blue Velvet* the Yellow Man's suit contrasts with the red robins and garden poppies as well as the blue velvet of Dorothy's robe. This use of colour provides the audience with a visual reinforcement of the plot elements. A conscious decision was made to film *The Elephant Man* in black and white to give the film a sense of realism because of its Victorian setting. In *INLAND EMPIRE* the film employs a number of colour palettes – washed-out Poland, bright Hollywood, black and white, tinted – to contrast the various strands that follow the multiple forms of Nikki/Susan.

Lynch's films are all about movement, his original desire to see paintings move having held true throughout his career. The camera is generally controlled in his earlier films, with little handheld work, allowing for exacting compositions. His later work is far more fluid in its application of camera movements, and when he does employ static shots in a film such as *Rabbits* the effect is more startling. *The Straight Story* has many languid sweeping aerial shots of sky and fields, and contrasts with the manic pacing of *Wild at Heart* and *Lost Highway* where at times it can seem as though the camera itself is suffering the heady, breakneck schisms of the films' protagonists.

The mise-en-scène (literally the 'setting the scene') of any film presents the audience with the world in which the film is set – from the far distant planet Arrakis, to Victorian London or even sleepy Lumberton with its picket fences. Ranging from the apparently ordinary to the extreme, Lynch's films always feature immaculately designed mise-en-scène and often display similar themes, regardless of how disparate the settings may first appear. Wood and forests have always had an important part to play in the scenery. They represent freedom but also the fearful, the dark and the unknown. Forests are vast places of beauty and danger, the wind rustling the leaves is deeply evocative. This love of wood is also reflected in many of the films' designs, from the logging town of Lumberton to the Great Northern Hotel's native American inspired ambience, Fred's fine taste in furniture in *Lost Highway* (actually designed by Lynch, the house belongs to him) and in *Dune's* House Atreides with its naturalistic décor. Complementing and contrasting the natural environment, full of secrets, is that of industry, oppressive in many ways but offering progress amidst the coldness of its rusted textures. This love-hate relationship with the trappings of mechanisation probably harks back to Lynch's days in Philadelphia, when he was living in an industrial area and working as a printer. It is large, loud, dangerous and dirty, but at the same time fascinating and hypnotic, and modern life could not be sustained without it. Heavy machinery is often given screen time just so its aesthetics can be enjoyed while the sight of smoke-billowing chimneys gives a polluted beauty to the London of *The Elephant Man* and in the Harkonnen world of latticed metal and smog.

Although many of the films are set contemporaneously they never seem dated, indeed many feel timeless. Lynch rarely uses contemporary clothing or make-up, giving the work a design aesthetic that represents an idealised, half-remembered America. The tight sweaters and short skirts of *Twin Peaks'* schoolgirls were never in fashion, so never go out of fashion. Men wear suits or work clothes that do little to indicate when the film was set; in Dale Cooper's case it's FBI standard issue with little overt styling. The only giveaway that *Blue Velvet* was made in the 1980s lies with the make-up that Sandy's friends wear, and they are in the film for but a few seconds. Everything else is part of Lynch time, an other-when untainted by the pace of modern city living. In many respects, even in his modern films, there's a sense of 1950s nostalgia, of America's quieter states where time trundles by at its own rate, unfazed by fashion.

Lynch has a penchant for unusual props that form part of the overall art design, drawing the viewer into a world quite unlike their own. Even mundane items such as lamps – shooting upward light – and armchairs seem to follow a design code. Interior sets often seem familiar across Lynch's oeuvre, for example the zig-zag flooring and immaculately rippled curtains seen in *Eraserhead* and later in the Black Lodge in *Twin Peaks*. Many of his films make use of old or unusual microphones; *Blue*

Velvet, Mulholland Dr., the translating microphone in *Dune* all provide a visual clue that foregrounds the sound element and brings attention to the filming process. This goes a stage further in *Blue Velvet* when Ben grabs a lead lamp as surrogate microphone to mime *In Dreams*. Cameras, too, are used to recall the filming process in the mind of the viewer. In *Lost Highway* the Mystery Man intimidates Fred with his camera, and Fred has already been spooked by the filming of his own household. Cameras fill the sets of *On the Air, INLAND EMPIRE* and *Mulholland Dr.* The only time during the series of *Twin Peaks* that we ever see Laura alive is through James's video.

As we have seen, Lynch's use of mise-en-scène, composition and colour provides much of the mood and meaning, aesthetic choices that convey emotion and unease. However it is through editing that these images are given further life by juxtaposition and relation. Editing is crucial to the success of a film, determining pace and giving the audience clues as to narrative development. Lynch worked with the same editor for many years – Mary Sweeney. The overriding editorial look of a David Lynch film varies to reflect the emotions he is trying to elicit. In *Lost Highway* long, languid and brooding takes are intercut with extremely fast editing to provide the rapid pace at which Fred is travelling down the highway. Similarly *Wild at Heart* uses aural and visual editing to show the speed of Sailor and Lula's car as it tears across the country, the breaks in the road markings punctuating the pace and complementing the soundtrack. In contrast, the slow pacing for *The Straight Story* is highly unusual, especially for a modern film. These days everything has to be fast cut to appeal to a generation weaned on MTV and two-minute Internet clips, but Lynch manages to take the tempo down and still hold audience interest. Audiences expect an unhurried pace in a heritage adaptation but not in a contemporary film. The power of editing here allows a six-week journey to fit into less than two hours, but maintains a pace that gives an accurate sense of the (lack of) speed of Alvin's journey. There are many events, lots happening in the narrative and several characters to get to know, but it doesn't feel like it.

Perhaps the most audacious slowing down of time through editing occurs at the start of the second series of *Twin Peaks*. Following the unbearable climax of the first season Lynch opened with a feature length episode that was alienating, frustrating and brilliant. Rather than resolve the multitude of cliff-hangers, he produced twelve interminable minutes of Cooper, wounded and immobile from his gunshot wound, negotiating a glass of milk with a geriatric waiter and receiving cryptic riddles from a Scandinavian giant. In retrospect, this is a wonderfully restrained piece of comedy that rewards with each subsequent visit, but on first viewing it is excruciating.

Film is about the elasticity of time, an idea that Lynch enjoys playing with. As a visual stylist he has few equals, understanding as he does the way that all the elements of a film's aesthetic can combine to produce a unified vision.

UNLOCK THE DREAM, SOLVE THE CRIME – MYSTERIES AND SECRETS

Jeffrey: I'm seeing something that was always hidden. I'm involved in
a mystery. I'm learning. And it's all secret.
Sandy: You like mysteries that much?
Jeffrey: Yeah. You're a mystery. I like you. Very much.

Film narratives are designed to pique an audience's interest primarily
through conflict and revelation. Conflict is at the heart of simpler narrative forms – the Hollywood action blockbuster for example – and easier
to understand. Revelation is a step removed, created through the need
to discover, not merely resolve, and it requires the audience to think,
sometimes even as the on-screen characters do. This is the mode of
storytelling that most interests David Lynch – revelation through the
unravelling of mysteries and secrets.

The traditional mystery film, the Conan Doyle/Agatha Christie narrative model, sees a crime committed and a solution sought. The detective involved isn't necessarily an authoritative figure, such as a
policeman, but such figures are often present in the story – and not
always to aid the main protagonist. *Twin Peaks* begins ostensibly as a
murder mystery, with its primary investigator Special Agent Dale
Cooper, the authoritative detective. But others also work the case:
James, Donna, Maddy and Audrey, the young amateur sleuths. An analogous premise occurs in *Blue Velvet* with Jeffrey and Sandy's recre-
ational detective work contrasting with the police operation's more

traditional investigative methods. The differences are quite striking: the young are always innocent but curiosity leads them down dark paths, whilst the police are professional because it's their job. In *Blue Velvet* these authority figures can prove to be corrupt, as evil as they are good. In *Twin Peaks* Cooper's calling to his profession bears signs of a youthful curiosity, which has subsequently led him to early career success. A similar calling resulted in his one-time partner Wyndom Earl pursuing an altogether darker path, the yin and yang of the esoteric FBI.

Twin Peaks and *Blue Velvet* are, in many ways, traditional mystery stories told from a skewed angle, one in which amateurs and professionals work towards the same goal using different methods, often on different sides of the moral divide. *Mulholland Dr.* and *INLAND EMPIRE* take this a step further. They are mysterious mysteries, in which a potentially criminal event has occurred but the crime, if there is one, is a mystery itself. The key to *Mulholland Dr.'s* first mystery – who is Rita? – is a case of identity discovery, the twist being that one of the investigators is the person they are investigating. But the film goes deeper because the possessions found on the amnesiac Rita indicate that a crime may have been involved. The biggest mystery is finding out what other mysteries there are to be solved. In Rita's case this could mean the discovery that she is not a good person. *INLAND EMPIRE* explores events surrounding a cursed film where the original actors were murdered. This leads to further mysteries and the complications surrounding actress Nikki's professional life, private life and psyche. Similarly *Lost Highway* begins with a basic, if creepy, mystery – who is sending Renee and Fred videotapes of their apparently secure house and why? – and soon spirals into several overlapping mysteries involving multiple personalities, murder and deceit.

'Sometimes a wind blows and the mysteries of love come clear.'

Mysteries don't have to revolve around the process of solving a crime or potential crime. As Jeffrey says, 'You're a mystery. I like you. Very much'. There are mysteries all around us and the biggest, the greatest, is love. It's the one mystery that binds characters as diverse as John Merrick, Albert Rosenfield, and Sailor and Lula. Although much of Lynch's work is dark – 'negative things like anger and depression and sorrow, they are beautiful things in a story'[26] – the heart of all this anger and conflict is often about unravelling the mysteries of love. That love does not conquer all but ascends triumphantly into the heavens is another existential mystery that shrouds Lynch's work. The closing of *Fire Walk With Me* shows the love of a father and daughter reunited despite incestuous violence that has led ultimately to their deaths. The mysteries of love lie in forgiveness and peace; enlightenment is the result of striving, of unlocking a wider consciousness.

The influence of surrealism in Lynch's work cannot be overlooked. The fundamental understanding of the term can be seen as the unravelling of dreams and dreamlike logic. In the world of David Lynch the border between the waking world and the unconscious one is often breached, a cinematic equivalent of Dali's *Dream Caused by the Flight of a Bee around a Pomegranate, a Second before Waking Up* (1944). Mysteries in the waking world and the unravelling of dreams are tightly intertwined, and in more than just a Freudian or Jungian way. They are often relational or cryptic, messages to be decoded, secrets. Dreams invade the waking world and the language of dreams becomes one that helps characters make sense of their environment and predicament – it allows them, and the audience, to unravel the meaning of what is around them. Dreams don't have to make rational sense in the cold light of day, they just have to feel right emotionally. This is the key to unlocking the secrets they contain. They have their own internal logic that relates to the real world, even if it is entirely separate or disparate from it, even if it is fragmented and disjointed, non-linear or confusing. Unlocking the secrets of dreams is key to the development of Paul Atreides in *Dune*; unravelling the dream allows him to form a rebellion, gain power and ultimately become the Kwisatz Haderach. Similarly Cooper's dream in *Twin Peaks* is central to the entire series and the film *Fire Walk With Me*; the meanings that are contained in one short sequence resonate throughout the whole show, peeling layers away as more of its secrets materialise. The creatures that inhabit the worlds outside of ours seep in through the cracks, becoming part of waking reality. The old couple in *Mulholland Dr.* and the fungus-covered bum behind Winkies' Diner inhabit a space 'between two worlds'.

Mulholland Dr., Lost Highway and *INLAND EMPIRE* have been interpreted as dreams – Betty dreaming at a number of points in the film, including the title sequence, or Fred flashing back on his life at the moment of execution, a blur of confused and contradictory memories, or indeed any of Nikki's multiple personalities. Where Lynch differs from many other filmmakers is that his dream states and waking states can co-exist. Henry's dreams invade his world to the point where its denizens are as real as Mary X and his child. In *The Grandmother* the fantasised grandmother is real, part of the boy's waking dream, but ignored by his parents. Dreams play such a part in *Twin Peaks* that their interpretation is brought out in the open – rather than just requiring the viewer to analyse the dream, it is also analysed within the film, intrinsically bound to the plot. Instead of supplying one explanation of a dream, as in Alfred Hitchcock's *Spellbound* (1945), the world of *Twin Peaks* seeks to delve beneath each of the layers of a dream to determine different solutions. *Spellbound* uses the language of psychiatry to explain the meaning of dream symbols because the film is about the psychiatric process, and the revelation of a secret that has been repressed by a disturbed patient provides the solution to the film. In the worlds of David Lynch, as with Freudian psychiatry, the repression hides multiple meanings, each solution revealing further mysteries. Making sense of the dreams in *Mulholland Dr.* or *Twin Peaks* results in the discovery of further secrets, not just a solitary solution.

The waking dream is generally a secret for the character to unravel – be it Paul Atreides' attempt to work out his destiny or Dale Cooper's to glean the meaning of the Giant's mysterious utterances following his shooting. These waking dreams, occurring on the borders between the dream world and the material world, have just as many layers but are initially less cryptic because their primary messages are solved transparently in the narrative. The Giant's clues – 'there is a man in a smiling bag' and 'without chemicals he points' – are solved and explained by Cooper as he slowly uncovers their meaning and begins to trust the messenger. This leads both us, and Cooper, to believe the Giant's secrets are easy to interpret given the right circumstances, but like any dream secret there are more depths to delve into. Like Lil's dance in *Fire Walk With Me* the superficial questions are basically riddles. The deeper secrets lie elsewhere. 'The question is – where have you gone?' turns out, along with 'The owls are not what they seem', to be the more pertinent conundrums offered by the Giant and the springboard for the entire second series. Like Cooper's dream, though, we are never made fully aware of the extent of the secrets contained in the Giant's speech as each revelation ultimately poses more mysteries.

One of the main examples in which the language of dreams is used in the real world is in *Fire Walk With Me* where Lil, the sour faced communicator of FBI boss Gordon Cole, gives a coded message to two Special Agents. Unravelling Lil's communication gives the audience as well as the detectives a grounding in how to interpret the secrets and mysteries not only of this film but of all Lynch's waking dream conundrums. Again, though, not all the layers are revealed. Despite the fact we have illustrated explanations of Lil's messages there is still more to fathom, in this case the meaning of the blue rose. Everything seen has meaning beyond surface interpretation; secrets are revealed only by freeing conscious thought, exploring the wider possibilities, however obtuse. Not only secrets themselves but the language of secrecy pervades: 'Laura was full of secrets' (*Twin Peaks*), 'I'll tell you a little secret – I want to die' (*Blue Velvet*), 'I know the secret. The worm is the spice…' (*Dune*), 'We all got a secret side, baby' (*Wild at Heart*). Each questions how much the audience and the characters really know.

In *Mulholland Dr.* the public exasperation about the film's meaning led Lynch down an unprecedented path. Always reluctant to discuss the meaning of his films – they are, after all, journeys of discovery where outside interpretation can destroy the joy of piecing together the puzzle for oneself – Lynch published ten keys to unlocking its secrets. The questions that he suggests the viewer asks – 'Pay attention in the beginning: two clues are revealed before the credits' and 'Where is Aunt Ruth?' – range from the apparently banal to the unanswerable or plain indecipherable. In pointing us towards certain additional pieces of information, Lynch allows us to view the film in a meta-light of revised emphasis, armed with insider knowledge from the filmmaker. Yet ultimately nothing he suggests can illuminate further that contained within the film – the material is that of emphasis, not of additional revelation. The result is simply a further layer of secrets. If people greeted *Mulholland Dr.* with confused admiration, the reception for the similarly elliptical *INLAND EMPIRE* was on occasion vitriolic, denouncing it as three hours of impenetrable nonsense. However, despite the fact that it doesn't give up its secrets easily, it is a coherent and thoroughly engaging film; and isn't it so much better to be able to question and debate the intricacies of the plot and the mysteries held within?

Film at its best is about wonder and discovery, of entering new worlds. Uncovering the unknown allows us to experience a child-like wonder even in the heart of the nightmare. Mysteries and secrets allow us to participate in the film, solving puzzles and empathising with the characters. Conflict exists to relate the audience to the screen on a purely visceral level, secrets entice the emotional and intellectual responses that can make cinema so rewarding and, sometimes, infuriating. In dreams he talks to you but through secrets he engages with you.

BILLY WAS HALFWAY BETWEEN HIS HOUSE AND THE SICKENING GARDEN OF LETTERS – LYNCH AND SURREALISM

'We are going to have the privilege tonight of witnessing some of the most unusual films ever produced.'[27]

For the purpose of this chapter the term 'Surrealist film' covers not only the work of the Surrealist directors but also of other filmmakers whose works are predominantly experimental or abstract in nature, whose films contain elements of the surreal. For example, whilst few people would describe Dziga Vertov as a Surrealist director (at the time it was argued he was a socialist realist), his work does contain abstractions and symbolic juxtaposition that are analogous to that of the surreal film.

Aside from the pioneering years of cinema at the opening of the twentieth century, filmmaking by its nature has fed upon itself in order to find a language and a structure. Few filmmakers truly work in a vacuum, unaffected by other artists. Lynch is no exception. Films like *The Elephant Man*, *The Straight Story* and *Blue Velvet* – however seemingly different – would make little sense on the screen if they didn't apply at least some of the trappings of the conventional Hollywood approach to narrative cinema. It could be argued that the power of *Mulholland Dr.*, *Lost Highway* or *Twin Peaks: Fire Walk With Me* is precisely that the confines of the accepted methods of filming are depicted first – then the audience is presented with subversive

Surrealist elements. The same is true in literature. The nihilistic Dadaist nonsense texts are in essence self-destructive; they need to exist but in many ways cannot evolve because their purpose is to be meaningless or at least absurd. For something to exist outside of strict formulaic confines there needs to be a balance between convention and subversion, form and deconstruction.

In many respects this places David Lynch as the natural successor to European directors such as Fellini or Buñuel in balancing the absurd and subversive with the structured and conservative. Lynch's surreal imagery resonates because it has an emotional intensity that is centred on characters that are constructed, at least in some ways, on the inherent filmic conventions of establishing and empathising. Laura Palmer's descent into nightmare, Henry's dreams, Paul Atreides' visions, Nikki's multiple personalities or Fred's metamorphosis into Pete would lack their emotional and visceral resonance if they were not in some way rooted in the trappings of conventional narrative cinema. What is perhaps more interesting is what happens when Lynch departs from strictly narrative devices and enters the dream worlds that, to many, typify his work. His influences depart significantly from any accepted Hollywood conventions but are not without precedence; experimental film is as old as cinema itself and Lynch is the tradition's most high-profile successor.

'If surrealism is the subconscious speaking, I think I identify with it... I am very happy to be a fellow traveller with any of these guys.'[28]

Surrealism is not just a disingenuous collection of odd images but rather a way of expressing the unconscious mind. The movement emerged around the time that psychoanalysis was evolving and it is no coincidence that the two apparently disparate movements find much of their energies consumed by dreams and the nature of dreaming. Surrealism is the rejection of conventional cause-effect logic in favour of dream logic, the argument that dreams make sense if you can interpret them correctly. As such they are mysteries or secrets to be unlocked – as Dale Cooper succinctly puts it, 'unlock the dream, solve the crime'. This is a departure from purely representational art (that looks also to a pre-representational art world of symbolism). Meaning isn't tied up purely in the literal understanding of the image. It relies in part on an emotional response to the image as much as an objective one. The Surrealist painters attempted to portray this logic of dreams on canvas but, like the emerging Cubist movement, they were also intrigued by the nature of time. Cubism attempted in part to deal with time distilled in a single moment, another departure from the snap-shot 'instance' of representational and realist art. Indeed when Marcel Duchamp partly revisited his painting *Nude Descending a Staircase* in the short film *Discs* he showed the image multiplied on the screen and animated, manifold timeframes also moving in time. When the Surrealists wanted to examine time they occasionally turned to another emerging artform – the cinema. Cinema offered possibilities to alter time, to make it elastic, and also to realise dreams more as they appear, as moving entities. Lynch's first foray into film came from a desire to see paintings move, the same spur that made the Surrealists turn to film.

The effect of the Surrealist and experimental film on the feel of Lynch's own work is profound. The title of Hans Richter's attempt to bring art cinema to the mainstream *Dreams that Money Can Buy* (1947) – marketed as Surrealist Freudian film – could very well apply to the whole of Lynch's oeuvre. In this film a man discovers that he can project dreams to people and sets up a business selling them. The dreams, introduced by a narrator over non-mouthing actors reminiscent of *Mulholland Dr.*'s Silencio Club scene, are provided by a number of artists and filmmakers to create an unusual portmanteau piece. The dreamseller's clients are named by individual letters (like Mrs A) recalling the X family in *Eraserhead* as well as the psychoanalytic practice of referring to patients, protecting their anonymity. In Man Ray's segment *Ruth, Roses and Revolver* – also the title of a BBC documentary in which Lynch introduced a number of Surrealist influences, many from this compilation – an audience are presented with a participatory and absurd film by a woman bearing a striking resemblance to Dorothy in *Blue Velvet*. The familiar red curtain and the act of watching and staging that occurs in a number of Lynch's films can be seen here. The foregrounding of the audience as part of the spectacle has resonance in *The Elephant Man*'s pantomime, Julee Cruise's performance in *Twin Peaks* and the disjointed, fake interaction of *Rabbits*. The nature of viewing an audience brings home the artificiality of cinema. After all, the 'audience' we are watching is just as manufactured as the on-screen antics they are engaging with. The segment ends by revealing the date of authorship – 1950 – a good four years after the film was made.

In film, time is elastic to the point of destruction. Hans Richter's *Narcissus*, while recalling the Dali sequence in Hitchcock's *Spellbound*, features a blue man isolated in an increasingly chaotic and frightening world. It's not a huge stretch of the imagination to relate him to the Yellow Man or even to the multiple personalities of *Lost Highway* and *Mulholland Dr.* when he utters the words, 'One day in May it suddenly happened. I met myself'. Max Ernst's *Desire* segment features several elements that are reminiscent of Lynch's work – the emerging golden ball from the heroine's mouth recalls *Eraserhead* and the visions of Paul Atreides. The extreme close-ups and unusual fetishised camera angles recall Dorothy in *Blue Velvet*. Also, under her bed lurks evil, waiting to pull her down, like Laura Palmer cowering before a menacing Bob. While *Dreams that Money Can Buy* goes some way to differentiate between the dream and wakened states, Lynch, together with most of the Surrealist film directors, does not permit so concrete a distinction, allowing the dream world instead to invade the waking one and contaminate it. In dreams there are codes and meanings that need deciphering to make sense of the imperfections of the waking world.

Dreams form a key to understanding the world. The FBI of *Twin Peaks* are all too aware of this. Dale Cooper relies on dreams to provide him with clues. The creatures from the Black Lodge skirt the boundaries between the waking and sleeping worlds. Events are not meant to be

Isabella Rossellini in *Blue Velvet*

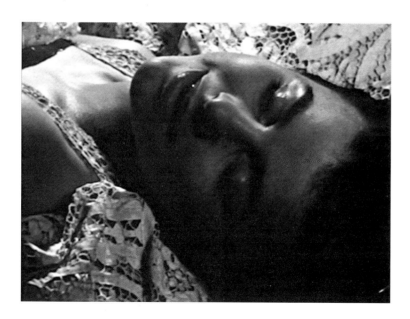

Max Ernst's *Desire* from *Dreams that Money Can Buy*

taken literally but symbolically. In the Buñuel and Dali films *Un Chien Andalou* and *L'Age d'Or* (1930) we are meant to infer and interpret from the visual information we are given – the films attack on an emotional and intuitive level rather than a purely intellectual one. Accepted narrative film language dictates that editing and visual information indicate associative meaning but in the world of the Surrealist filmmaker the meaning is symbolic not direct. Leland's metamorphosis to Bob and back can only really be understood on an emotional level, for Bob inhabits another world, distinct from ours but connected to it. He is as much symbolic as he is real. Similarly in *Un Chien Andalou* what we see is symbolic – the 'ants in the hand' a play on words, the severed hand a representational clitoris, the priests the moral burden of religious indoctrination holding back the protagonist's sexual desires. Buñuel uses subjective imagined points of view to disorientate the viewer; conventional cinema shows us the 'reality' of a subject's viewpoint to establish empathy with the character. In *Un Chien Andalou* we are shown the man's imaginary point of view when he corners the heroine and fondles her breasts. In his mind she is naked when in fact she is fully clothed. Similarly in *Lost Highway* we are shown Pete's subjective memory of Alice rather than the actuality of the event. Many other occurrences in *Un Chien Andalou* have resonances in Lynch's work – the falling in one place to arrive in another (*Mulholland Dr., INLAND EMPIRE*), the dark in the forests. Indeed the discovery of a man's body in the wood echoes the shot at the opening of *Premonitions Following an Evil Deed*.

As with much art, surrealism is often associated with sexual thought – indeed its relationship to psychoanalysis required it to be a movement that concerned itself with sexuality. Themes of masochistic sexuality pepper the texts of *Mulholland Dr., Blue Velvet* and *Lost Highway* in much the same way that Jean Cocteau approaches homoerotic masochism in his semi-autobiographical *Le Sang d'un poète* (1930). Cocteau breaks down the walls between the waking world and the dream world, just as Lynch does in *Twin Peaks* when Cooper enters the Black Lodge. There is a transitional phase. In *Le Sang d'un poète* this is

achieved via an incredible effect where the hero litera
through a mirror, entering a bizarre world where the laws c
stretched, and all aspects of normality turned on their hea
fixation on statues, a theme he would return to in his films, r
La Belle et la bête (1945), can be seen in the statues that are conspicu-
ously isolated in the scenery of the Black Lodge. Cocteau's use of
reverse film to create a sense of the otherworldly is evident in the backwards talking in Twin Peaks and the stilted surrealism of Lynch's advert
for Parisienne cigarettes. A more playful use of reversed film to create a
feeling of absurdity rather than disassociation can be seen in René Clair
and Francis Picabia's Entr'acte (1924) and in Hans Richter's
Vormittagsspuk (1927). It is worth noting that, despite the humour in
some of these films, at the time they were considered to be as controversial as anything Lynch has produced;, indeed Richter's film was
banned as subversive, placing the filmmaker under considerable
scrutiny.

A mystery man, invasions into your home by unknown persons and
damn fine coffee – Maya Deren and Alexander Hammid's Meshes of the
Afternoon (1943) has echoes of Dale Cooper's nightmare dash through
a labyrinthine Black Lodge, with keys opening ever spiralling worlds of
Mulholland Dr. and the fractured duplicated personalities and warped
time structure of Lost Highway. The similarities between Deren's film
and Lynch's worlds are quite pronounced: a record clicks rhythmically at
the end of its play, strange shadows appear on the walls, people follow
copies of themselves and Russian dolls of keys compound the
mysteries within. Stylised drones on the soundtrack create a sense of
unease and apparently diegetic sounds emphasise emotional meaning
but do not match our expectations of on-screen events.

The abstract film has less obvious impact on Lynch's cinema but
nevertheless feeds into the general ambience of his work. Fernand
Léger's Ballet mécanique and The Girl with the Pre-Fabricated Heart
(from Dreams that Money Can Buy) show similar obsessions with the
artificial, industrial, electrical and mechanical – the textures of industry

offering a strange and abstract beauty. The latter's romance between two shop mannequins is made sinister by their obvious rigidity, lack of humanity and the film's overly quirky soundtrack. As Lynch puts it, 'Anything that looks human but isn't looks frightening'[29], a comment that could be levelled at many of his creations from the baby in *Eraserhead* to the denizens of the Black Lodge. But Lynch's films are always about the human in the industrial, the pull between industry and nature, a kind of nightmarish Thomas Hardy. Rhythm, the love and fear of machinery, and the juxtaposition of man and mechanics can be seen in Dziga Vertov's abstract documentary *Man with a Movie Camera* (1929), a dizzying montage of images that shows a day in the life of a Russian city. Meant as a democratic celebration of the proletariat, these days the film comes across as a wonderfully manipulative and dazzling example of abstract and relational montage as the rhythm and pounding intensity of industry is expressed in purely visual terms.

While little of Lynch's work has the raw intensity of *Man with a Movie Camera*, he nevertheless displays a similar awe for the industrial process and its abstraction, particularly in his photographic work, which owes much to Vertov's lauding of industrialism as abstract art. Texture, repeated superimposition and the abstract shapes offered by speeding camerawork can be seen in Man Ray's cinepoems *Emak-Bakia* (1926) and *L'Étoile de Mer* (1928). The latter's combination of the heavens, dangerously seductive women and raging flames seems to resonate in the worlds of *Wild at Heart* and *Lost Highway*.

'How exciting it must have been to have been a filmmaker in the early days of cinema, because not only was it so magical to see paintings begin to move, but they could start altering time...'[30]

Like many of the twentieth century's pioneering artists Lynch works in a number of media – painting, sculpture, photography, installation work, art experiments and, of course, film. These are different but not unconnected disciplines, and much of his output comes from a tradition of surrealism that includes film work from artists whose traditional skills have often been held in higher regard. The fact that their films are less appreciated doesn't diminish their importance – the influence of the Surrealist filmmakers on David Lynch's work, in the cinema and elsewhere, cannot be overlooked.

ENDNOTES

Unless attributed here, all quotations came from the particular work discussed in the commentary.

1   Jeffrey Beaumont (Kyle MacLachlan), *Blue Velvet*
2   David Lynch, *The Guardian*, Jan 12 2002
3   Ibid
4   David Lynch quoting Mel Brooks, *Lynch on Lynch*, Chris Rodley (ed), Faber & Faber, 1997, p93
5   David Lynch, *The Guardian*, Jan 12 2002
6   David Lynch, *Lynch on Lynch*, Chris Rodley (ed), Faber & Faber, 1997, p193
7   David Lynch, *Sunday Times,* Jan 6 2002
8   David Lynch, *Variety,* May 11 2005
9   David Lynch, Introduction to *Six Figures Getting Sick*, The Short Films of David Lynch DVD, Absurda, 2005
10 David Lynch, Introduction to *The Alphabet*, The Short Films of David Lynch DVD, Absurda, 2005
11 David Lynch, *Lynch on Lynch*, Chris Rodley (ed), Faber & Faber, 1997, p69
12 Kyle MacLachlan, *The Making of Dune*, WH Allen and Co, 1984, p44
13 David Lynch quoting Daniel Toscan du Plantier, Introduction to *The Cowboy and the Frenchman*, The Short Films of David Lynch DVD, Absurda, 2005
14 Le Blanc and Odell, *David Lynch*, Pocket Essentials, 2003, p42
15 Barry Gifford, *Hotel Room Trilogy,* 1993, Preface
16 David Lynch, Introduction to *Premonitions Following an Evil Deed*, The Short Films of David Lynch DVD, Absurda, 2005
17 David Lynch, *Variety*, May 12, 2005
18 Laura Dern, http://www.thecityofabsurdity.com/
19 Harley Peyton, *Wrapped In Plastic* No 17, 1995, p6
20 David Lynch, *Lynch on Lynch*, Chris Rodley (ed), Faber & Faber, 1997, p217

21 David Lynch, davidlynch.com

22 David Lynch, David Lynch Foundation http://www.davidlynchfoundation.com/tour/
index.html, Oct 2005

23 David Lynch, David Lynch Foundation http://www.davidlynchfoundation.com/
message.html, Oct 2005

24 David Lynch, David Lynch Foundation http://www.davidlynchfoundation.com/tour/
index.html, Oct 2005

25 David Lynch, *Newsweek*, 26 July 2005

26 David Lynch, David Lynch Foundation http://www.davidlynchfoundation.com/
tour/index.html, Oct 2005

27 *Ruth, Roses & Revolver*, Man Ray, from *Dreams that Money Can Buy*

28 David Lynch, *David Lynch Presents Ruth, Roses & Revolver*, BBC Arena, 1987

29 Ibid

30 Ibid

BIBLIOGRAPHY

Butler, Andrew M, *Film Studies*, Pocket Essentials, Harpenden, 2002

Chion, Michel, *David Lynch*, British Film Institute, London, 1995

Frost, Scott, *Agent Cooper: My Life, My Tapes,* Penguin Books, USA, 1991

Gifford, Barry, *Hotel Room Trilogy*, University Press of Mississippi, 1995

Gifford, Barry, *The Wild Life of Sailor and Lula*, Rebel Inc, Edinburgh, 1998

Hughes, David, *The Complete Lynch*, Virgin Books, London, 2001

Kaleta, Kenneth C, *David Lynch* (Twayne's Filmmakers Series), Twayne, 1992

Le Blanc, Michelle & Odell, Colin, *David Lynch*, Pocket Essentials, Harpenden, 2003

Lynch, David & Frost, Mark, *The Access Guide to Twin Peaks*, Pocket Books, 1991

Lynch, David & Gifford, Barry, *Lost Highway*, Faber & Faber, London, 1997

Lynch, David & Rodley, Chris, *Lynch on Lynch*, Faber & Faber, London, 1997

Lynch, Jennifer, *The Secret Diary of Laura Palmer*, Penguin Books, USA, 1992

Miller, Craig & Thorne, John (editors), *Wrapped in Plastic Magazine 12–18*, Win-Mill
    Productions, Arlington, 1994–95

Naha, Ed, *The Making of Dune*, WH Allen and Co, Berkshire, 1984

Nochimson, Martha P, *The Passion of David Lynch: Wild at Heart in Hollywood,*
Univ of Texas Pr, 1997

Woods, Paul A, *Weirdsville USA: The Obsessive Universe of David Lynch,*
Plexus, London, 1997

INDEX